First published in 2012 by
Vivien Twyford Communication Pty Limited
Trading as Twyfords Consulting

© Vivien Twyford Communication Pty Limited

ISBN: 978-0-646-57916-0

Vivien Twyford, Stuart Waters, Max Hardy, John Dengate

The Power of 'Co' :
The Smart Leaders' Guide to Collaborative Governance

Cover Design by Matthew Hardy
Text design and layout by Weston & Co Publishers
Edited by Owen Thomson, Encore Communications
Printed by Weston & Co Publishers

Dedicated to all our clients who,
over the years, have taught us
the power of collaboration.

CONTENTS

Introduction
THE POWER OF 'CO'

> *"Change is disturbing when it's done to us;*
> *it's exhilarating when it's done by us."*
>
> Elisabeth Moss Kanter

Have you noticed how many words start with the prefix 'co' in the English language? Consider this quick baker's dozen: c*oordinate, cooperate, contribute, consult, connect, compromise, communication, common, commitment, collective, cohesion, collaboration* and *coefficient*. They all relate in some way to people working together effectively.

That's the Power of 'Co' – the term we have coined for this book and for the focus of our work.

These humble two letters can be added to almost any action word to demonstrate powerfully that the activity is being done by a number of people working together to achieve an agreed and shared outcome. Thus, you will see that the work we are describing in this book incorporates many verbs (or doing words) starting with 'co', in particular, *collaborate, commit, co-define, co-design, co-create, co-generate, co-deliver, coordinate, cooperate* and *communicate*.

'Co', the dictionary tells us, means *'with'*. So, *'Co-define'* means defining something together with others. *'Co-design'* means sharing the design process in a way that allows many to contribute to it. *'Co-create'* means a process of shared creation where two or more people interact within the creative process. *'Co-efficient'* means adding a multiplier effect to something to achieve a more illuminated view of the problem as well as a more creative outcome. *'Co-deliver'* means sharing in the delivery or implementation of a decision. All of these *'co'* activities require commitment, communication,

coordination and cooperation with contributions from a collective group to achieve a common understanding and a co-generation of innovative possibilities as a result of a collaborative process. Whew! The Power of 'Co'!

In order to describe what we mean by the Power of 'Co' we will now relate four stories. They demonstrate that collaboration, as the practical form of 'co', where people work together to share problems and find enduring solutions, is alive and well, at least here in Australia and New Zealand.

Four stories of Co:-
NSW Southern Highlands, 2006 - Wingecarribee Shire Council

Wingecarribee Shire Council, a small council in New South Wales, needed approval from the State Government for something known as a Special Rate Variation. This meant providing evidence that council rates needed to be increased by more than a permitted rate peg and demonstrating that the rate-paying community was generally supportive of the increase. After failing to achieve a rate rise in 2005, Council approached Twyfords the following year to facilitate a meeting with its community to seek approval.

We proposed something different from the one-off public information session that had failed to convince ratepayers in previous years. Instead, we suggested two public meetings a week apart with a unique additional ingredient in the middle.

At the first meeting, information was provided on the current state of infrastructure and the challenge of maintaining it without a significant increase in rates. Participants were unconvinced and, as anticipated, did not support a rate increase. However, our additional ingredient was the formation of a small working party to better understand Council's dilemma. Volunteers were invited to take part. About a dozen people (the most passionate and articulate community leaders) put their hands up.

The working party spent the first part of the day on a mini-bus inspecting roads and bridges that needed repairing, netball courts that were cracked, and playgrounds that were unsafe. Then they examined Council's books. Council engineers explained how rate money is spent, why much of the area's existing infrastructure was currently unsafe and what maintaining infrastructure actually costs. At the end of the day the group was asked: "What have you learned and what can we agree on?"

The group told their stories at the second public meeting. One gentleman said, "I reckon we should go for this rate rise because it's really important to us." By the end of the second meeting most participants had a clear picture of Council's dilemma and the need for a Special Rate Variation. They appreciated being invited into the problem rather than being sold a solution.

Auckland, 2006 – Transit New Zealand

We were asked to undertake a peer review of a citywide consultation strategy in New Zealand's largest city. Transit New Zealand was then the national road authority and had recognised that, in order to solve some of Auckland's major traffic issues, a new motorway was needed. While parts of the new western motorway had already been built, there were still connecting pieces requiring significant funding.

Transit proposed completing the whole route by 2015 and paying back borrowings through a tolling scheme. Without funding from tolls the completion date would be delayed to 2030. New Zealand law required public support to be demonstrated before approval for tolling could be granted.

Our peer review recommended more than Transit's typical consultation process of information documents, submissions and public hearings. We felt the Auckland public needed to understand the dilemma facing Auckland transport planners, the solutions considered, the value in time saved that the new motorway would provide as well as alternative methods of funding.

We recommended that Transit incorporate some deliberative elements into their process, facilitating understanding of the planning and funding issues. One hundred people from each of four geographic areas of Auckland (North, Central, West and South) were invited to attend two sessions held two weeks apart in their area. Participants were presented with information about the dilemma and the tolling proposal and then divided into small groups with a facilitator, maps and documents. They asked questions and sought explanations.

Technical experts from Transit were available to answer questions. Each participant, at the end of the session, was asked to explain what they had learned to at least three people, such as a family member, a work colleague, or a neighbour before they returned in two weeks. Explaining to others helped them identify what they still didn't understand.

At the second session they continued their conversations about the value of the new road and the tolling proposal. Only after their understanding had increased were participants asked to complete a questionnaire. Their responses were analysed quite separately from those received from members of the wider community who had received the same written information but had not taken part in the deliberative sessions.

Responses from the broader Auckland community were polarised. People who spent a lot of time on the road said, "For God's sake, just build this road, get it done, we'll pay tolls if that's what it takes." Alternatively those for whom faster travel was not important said, "Tolls? Not likely! Don't you dare!" However, the 400 people who had been part of the citywide engagement process provided comments such as: "Yes, we understand the dilemma. We think overall the motorway is a good solution for Auckland's traffic. We see the value in saving travelling time. We would like it completed earlier rather than later. We're not sure about tolling. We think you should investigate other ways of funding, but if a tolling mechanism is the only way then we'd go along with it. It has merit."

From the technical and social information gathered by Transit about the tolling proposal, the Board decided that tolling was, in fact, not the best answer. The value of the motorway to road users was demonstrated, but with the cost of establishing a tolling system being significant, it was deemed more appropriate to employ other mechanisms of revenue-raising that already existed to fund construction.

Sao Paulo, Brazil, 1990 – Semco and Ricardo Semler

While this is not a story in which Twyfords was involved, we have been influenced by the fascinating story of how sharing a corporate dilemma with employees over 30 years ago delivered incredible results.

Told by internationally renowned Brazilian business guru Ricardo Semler in his 1993 book "Maverick", it's a story of how, by sharing a vision of what the company could be and by giving freedom to his staff to organise themselves to reach those goals, Semler increased his company's revenue from US$4 million in 1982 to US$212 million in 2003. He transformed his company through a revolutionary attitude towards staff. No more dedicated receptionists, desks or organisational charts. He encouraged employees first to commit to a shared vision for the company and then to suggest their own hours of work and their own salaries. Employees engaged together to develop strategy, learned each other's jobs and evaluated their boss' performance.

Semler related to his workers not as children to be persuaded, cajoled or managed, but as an asset to be invited to step up and be a part of solving a complex problem. He shared information on the health of the entire organisation so employees would have information on which to make decisions. He set up a profit-sharing system and insisted that the company's financials be published internally, so that everyone could see how the company was doing.

He surrendered the typical "command and control" power in order to achieve strong and sustainable outcomes. Contrary to all expectations, the workers didn't grant themselves unrealistic utopian conditions. Nor did they award themselves exorbitant pay rates. Rather, they employed a high degree of flexibility and were able to create enormous benefits and rewards for themselves and the business as a whole.

New Zealand, 2009-2010 – Land and Water Forum

In 2008, freshwater management was a significant issue in New Zealand, with the need to ascertain how competing interests could be balanced constituting a key concern.

In response, the NZ Minister for the Environment, Nick Smith, and the Minister of Agriculture and Forestry, David Carter, sought advice, seeking shared understanding of the issue and some agreement on a way forward so the Government could make sustainable, workable and enduring policy decisions.

The Land and Water Forum was established to conduct a stakeholder-led collaborative governance process to recommend reform of New Zealand's freshwater management through a consensus process.

The Chair of the Land and Water Forum, Alastair Bisley, described the Forum as an inclusive group of stakeholders committed to working together to find a consensus, and a government that supported them by giving them the space and the authority to do so.

At the end of August 2010 the Forum's core group of 21 main players, assisted by the six active observers from local and central government, reached consensus on a report which made 53 recommendations to reform freshwater management in New Zealand. The Plenary stakeholder group of another 60 participants from across the water spectrum agreed that this report should be sent at once to Ministers. Ministers Smith and Carter welcomed it formally in the Parliament Dining Hall and asked the Forum to share it at a series of public meetings around New Zealand.

What the stories tell us:

Our stories suggest that there is no one right way to create 'Co'. It's not a mechanistic approach where you can press a button and make it happen. 'Co' is about building relationships and trust. It's about people, the dilemmas they face and the conversations they need to have in order to understand the dilemma before trying to solve it.

As we explore the benefits 'Co' can bring, we increasingly recognise the need for specific conditions to be established before any benefits can be realised. These conditions particularly relate to the culture and mindsets within an organisation about the value of 'Co'.

For example, we have learned that for 'Co' to be successful, those involved have to believe (or at least be open to the possibility) that people are capable of moving past their own narrow self-interest, firstly to understand and secondly to find genuine solutions to social problems.

An effective leader is one who can identify when 'Co' is the most appropriate response to a complex problem or controversial dilemma and can build within their organisation both the conditions and the capacity for 'co'.

An effective leader knows that 'Co' can't be done to people. Everyone involved in solving the problem has to believe in the potential of 'Co' and commit to working together, first to understand the extent of the problem and then to agree on a process for making decisions. Only when trust has been developed between the parties through exploring common ground and agreeing on a framework for 'Co' can shared knowledge be brought together to co-create solutions that stick.

A process of 'Co' needs to be developed for each particular problem, each stakeholder group and each governance situation.

Collaborative Governance

We at Twyfords have developed a model of effective collaboration between stakeholders which we call Collaborative Governance. Our definition of Collaborative Governance is "a way of working with diverse stakeholders to co-create enduring solutions to society's most complex issues".

Collaborative Governance demands the sharing of both power and trust. It also requires a belief in people and their strengths, clear leadership and inclusive processes.

Collaborative Governance is in essence, *appreciative, informative, deliberative* and *iterative*.

Appreciative – focusing on strengths, abilities and energy of stakeholders to find enduring solutions to challenging problems;

Informative – encouraging conversations to share an understanding of all perspectives, to learn together and to build respect and trust between stakeholders;

Deliberative – sharing knowledge and working together to co-create new ideas and solutions that are informed, sustainable and enduring;

Iterative – starting at any point in a problem-solving or decision-making process but, like a seed being planted, needing the right environment and conditions in which to thrive.

The Power of 'Co' – the Book

This book is about Collaborative Governance, or the Power of 'Co'. This book provides real evidence of the benefits of collaboration (and all the other 'Co' words) as well as a theoretical framework on which to build the capacity of organisations and individuals to collaborate more often and more effectively to address dilemmas and find solutions that stick.

In **Chapter One** we look at the Power of 'Co' to create positive change in society by understanding what makes a problem complex and how to formulate an unprecedented, qualitatively different approach to creating enduring solutions.

In **Chapter Two** we explore the Paradox of Power and the challenge for today's leaders including elected representatives, corporate directors, executives, and in fact anyone with power to make decisions that affect others. We offer an explanation of the paradox and offer 'smart' power as a new approach. We contend that 'smart' power is shared power. We suggest that leaders who share their power, who co-create goals with their stakeholders, who share the dilemmas with those who can help solve them, and who provide a supportive environment in which problems can be solved collaboratively become leaders others wish to follow.

In **Chapter Three** we explain each step in the Collaborative Governance process and describe how these steps build the essential foundations of commitment, co-definition and co-design. We illustrate how they connect people to each other and build energy, trust, enthusiasm and cooperation to reach the ultimate goal of enduring solutions.

Chapters Four, Five, Six and **Seven** describe in detail each of the five steps of Collaborative Governance - a virtual roadmap for harnessing the Power of 'Co' in many different situations.

The last two chapters provide a summary and a list of resources and references that we have used in our work and drawn upon when writing this book.

We will be very interested to learn of any reactions you have to our work and invite you to send comments to any one of us at twyfords@twyfords.com.au.

Vivien Twyford, Max Hardy, John Dengate, Stuart Waters and Tania Jones
WOLLONGONG, APRIL 2012

Chapter 1

The Power of 'Co' to Create Positive Change

> *"Never doubt that a small group of thoughtful committed citizens can change the world; indeed, it's the only thing that ever has."*
>
> Margaret Mead

It only takes a casual glimpse of a TV news bulletin or daily newspaper headline to remind us that our world is a complex place. Issues like climate change, childhood obesity, tribalism leading to civil war and the plight of asylum seekers are just a handful of the complex issues demanding strong leadership, careful exploration and a wider understanding, as well as thoughtful, in-depth policy responses.

Instead we observe 'knee-jerk' reactions to loud vocal minorities; we listen to political leaders who seem to make policy on the run in an attempt to placate community dissent. We read inflammatory media pieces that seem eager to alienate and demonise alternate viewpoints. We see policy-making that appears to be based, at least in part, on the opinions of focus groups whose participants lack even a cursory understanding of the issues they're asked to comment on.

Lindsay Tanner, in his book *'Sideshow: Dumbing Down Democracy'*, says *"I am very pessimistic about the future of Australian politics, as the (media) sideshow syndrome seeps ever more insidiously into every tiny corner of government."* In the same book he quotes American political commentator Mark Bowden's observation on the drivers of ill-informed public opinion and subsequent political response: *"The public good is viewed only through a partisan lens and politics becomes blood sport,"* he says. *"Television loves this because it's dramatic - confrontation is all"*.

Symptoms of systemic problems

If we examine the ability of society to arrive at any type of meaningful and lasting solutions to these types of issues, it quickly becomes apparent that the unhelpful dynamic existing between the media and politicians creates a chronic unwillingness to fully appreciate issues that are inherently complex.

Instead, we end up with an emotionally-charged media approach featuring diametrically opposed positions that does much for TV ratings and website hits, but nothing in terms of educating or providing a platform for people to respond thoughtfully. This leads to a strengthening of positions at the polar ends of the spectrum with a corresponding unwillingness to understand different perspectives or move to higher ground.

Consequently, when a complex problem arises, people have no interest in exploring the underlying dilemma of the issue presented to them, instead being satisfied to align themselves with the one extreme side or perspective that they can easily relate to.

Furthermore, they exhibit little or no interest in exploring or seeking to understand the bigger picture, sometimes even studiously avoiding it altogether because it is perhaps too scary, too challenging or too overwhelming to contemplate.

For example, it seems much easier to categorise refugees seeking asylum in Australia as either potential terrorists or queue-jumpers sneaking into Australia to take our jobs and threaten our way of life. It seems to be too hard to make the effort or take the time to understand the underlying factors like war, poverty and persecution that drive people to undertake immensely risky courses of action. Greater understanding leads to a willingness to explore innovative ways to offer compassionate help to those who reach our shores that might benefit all Australians.

When attempts to arrive at a solution are driven by the results of focus groups or polling and decisions are made to achieve short-term political outcomes, the ability of leaders to inspire lasting solutions is sorely compromised and real progress on complex issues becomes impossible.

Lindsay Tanner provides an example about the Rudd government hearing powerful messages from focus groups of concern about the cost of living. He says, *"Inevitably, the truth beneath such concerns is very complex and difficult to deal with. The most important contributions that government can make ... are indirect and complicated. Productivity ... regulatory reforms, infrastructure investment and skill formation will eventually deliver higher living standards. But because this is difficult to explain . other approaches have to be pursued. These initiatives will usually have very marginal effects, but they generally sound good .... it looks like the government is doing something."*

What kind of problems are we talking about?

Terminology always presents a challenge in the work we do, with the literature giving us several labels with which to describe difficult social problems that require a new approach. One of these terms - "wicked problems" - was coined in 1973 and has been used to describe complex social problems that resist all attempts at resolution and seriously challenge the thinking of both policy-makers and policy implementers alike. We agree with the description of the problems, but not with the term chosen to describe them.

The predominantly negative use of the term 'wicked' may well influence how we orient ourselves to this kind of complex issue. The way we think influences the way we see the world and experience "reality". Perhaps a different term would help us experience the same problems differently; as opportunities for a new approach, rather than things to be overcome. We might value them more as opportunities for challenge, encouraging us to learn, to grow and to innovate together.

At Twyfords, we consider the term 'dilemma' to offer a better description and we have used that word extensively in this book, together with the term "complex problem" as described in the section that follows. The use of the word 'dilemma' becomes our contribution to the terminology debate.

Throughout this book we have used the terms "dilemma", "complex problem" and "controversial issue" almost interchangeably. We prefer the word "dilemma", as to us the term contains all the nuances of meaning inherent in the concept we are describing. However, we realise that for others the language of "problem to solve" and "issue to address" is more

---

descriptive. Whichever term resonates the meaning is the same. That meaning is clarified in the next few pages.

Examples of modern-day dilemmas

Consider the current high levels of childhood and adult obesity. Back in 1950 this wasn't a problem because lifestyle and food consumption habits were totally different to those practised now.

By contrast, today's marketplace is dominated by a multitude of unhealthy processed foods that are not only high in sugar and fat, but also high on the shopping lists of many Australians.

Consequently, the complex question has become: Who's responsible for our unhealthy population and how do we reduce obesity? In trying to find a solution we ask ourselves whether the fault lies with parents, schools, society, the government, the food industry, the advertising industry or simply the individual who eats unwisely or too much? Is it all or none of these? Is the solution to legislate, to educate or to punish? Or is it all or none of these?

Another example of increasing complexity is in the arena of local government. Twenty-five years ago local government included the responsibilities of 'roads, rates and rubbish'. Today the business of local government is vastly more complicated.

It requires understanding and managing an ageing population with changing expectations for services, less funding from federal and state governments, changing community demographics, conflicts between developers and communities over what is 'appropriate development', as well as the management of sophisticated budgets including maintenance of an ageing asset infrastructure.

New examples of complex issues facing 21st century societies include climate change, traffic congestion in cities, development of urban and suburban spaces and how to share equitably increasingly limited resources such as oil, energy, water and food.

When we examine such problems or dilemmas more closely they do appear to have definite and identifiable characteristics. Firstly, they are hard to define clearly. Indeed, there may be many different versions of the dilemma, with each version possessing an element or elements of truth. However, a single version may not represent the whole truth. It's even difficult to verify any version as right or wrong when it describes one aspect or facet of the dilemma which is true from a single perspective but not of the whole.

Dilemmas have many causes that are often interrelated and interdependent. Consequently, there is no single 'silver bullet' response. Any workable solution will require trade-offs and compromises as different people will have different priorities. Moreover, potential solutions will often be mutually exclusive, thus increasing the complexity of the challenge.

Additionally, attempts to find solutions to dilemmas produce unintended consequences, such as the creation of an equally undesirable alternative as a result of discouraging a particular unwanted behaviour. An old but useful example is the US authorities' introduction of Prohibition in the early part of the 20th century. Intended to reduce or eliminate alcohol consumption, it also resulted in a proliferation of organised crime. Initially focused on profiting from the high demand for illegal alcohol, these ventures soon evolved to incorporate a range of other illegal activities.

Frequently, modern dilemmas are dynamic and evolving, changing their size, scope and impacts too quickly for society to adjust to easily. Additionally, attempts to find solutions are often based on untested or unrealistic assumptions. Potential solutions are rarely verifiable as being right or wrong. Instead, they tend to be categorised as better, worse, or good enough. In short, there is no solution that guarantees a one hundred percent cure-all. Outcomes have to be negotiated, with even the best outcome not being something that will satisfy everyone.

Dilemmas are socially complex and solutions require coordinated actions from unrelated or unconnected organisations across different sectors. This is why they create so many problems for government, who frequently display a chronic inability to coordinate effectively or realistically across their own bureaucratic silos, let alone an ability to cooperate, coordinate or partner with non-government organisations. Attempts at brokering solutions are often associated with chronic policy failures over a period of many years. This need for cooperation is certainly not a recent problem, but something that keeps changing its shape as people try to solve it.

Dilemmas are associated with mistrust of those who have identified and defined the problem in a particular way and offer solutions that are based on technology or 'good' science. With lasting solutions mostly requiring the exercise of value judgments, it's simply not adequate to have a technical or scientific expert announce what the 'right' answer should be. For example, when considering climate change, almost everyone agrees that the planet is warming. Disagreement generally stems from different value judgements about what is causing the change and whether we should deal with it now or leave it to future generations.

A technical analysis will not address what people are experiencing emotionally or provide an adequate response to something they feel may be inherently unjust. For example, an agricultural scientist claiming that a particular mining project will not affect a community's agricultural land will do nothing to dispel feelings of mistrust and resentment of the mining company, nor will it influence the value judgement about whether particular land should be used to feed a community or provide raw materials for industry.

Another description of dilemmas

Another way of analysing and describing dilemmas is the Cynefin (pronounced Kin-ef-in) model, which describes and distinguishes between problems of a simple, complicated, complex and chaotic nature.

A simple problem, according to this model, is one where the solution already exists somewhere. Cause and effect is predictable and the appropriate

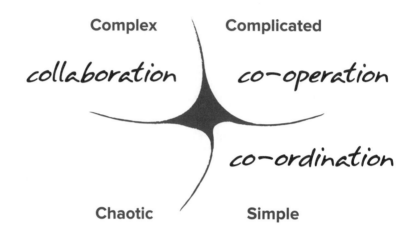

FIG. 1 – CYNEFIN MODEL

Complex — collaboration

Complicated — co-operation

co-ordination

Chaotic

Simple

Complex
Cause and effect may be identifiable in retrospect, but is unlikely to conform with prior expectations of how things work. Interventions must be flexible as outcomes may be unforseen.

Complicated
Cause and effect may be unclear at the time, but can be inferred using data, analysis and expert knowledge. Once understood, rules for intervention can be defined and followed.

Chaotic
Cause and effect relationships may be speculated in retrospect, but cannot be validated. Interventions must be approached as a learning exercise: act, sense then revise if necessary.

Simple
Cause and effect is predictable and the appropriate response to definable situations can be codified in Standard Operating Procedures which then drive interventions.

solution can be found in established procedures. Such problems can generally be solved by drawing on relevant knowledge created in the past.

For example, we know the damage that a car travelling at 30 kilometres per hour will incur when hitting a stationary object. The consequences of the impact will be predictable by the unwavering laws of physics and road rules have subsequently been created to help drivers recognise and avoid such eventualities. Co-ordination of knowledge and actions is what is needed to find solutions to simple problems.

Complicated problems are extensions of simple ones. While the solution may not be immediately known it can be established by examining known facts and past experience. For example, when a car engine malfunctions, an owner devoid of any expert mechanical knowledge may be unable to fix the problem, but can source either a single expert or multiple experts who will have the ability to solve it. Engineers, either alone or in groups, are very good at solving complicated technical problems because they have relevant knowledge and experience. Co-operation between experts is what is needed to find solutions to complicated problems.

A complex problem, the true heart of our dilemma, is qualitatively different. It stems from the reality that the known facts may not result in the same solution today or tomorrow as they did yesterday. You cannot predict the effect by examining the cause. Complex problems have similar characteristics to the dilemmas described in the previous section.

If complex problems, or dilemmas, are treated as if they were simple or even complicated it is likely that any solutions, if in fact they can be implemented, will be short-term at best and, at worst, will create unintended consequences that replace or even exceed those of the original problem. First identifying and then getting agreement on a course of action is a challenge. Implementing it and getting the desired outcomes is even more of a challenge.

Collaboration between all stakeholders to agree on the nature of the problem and then work together to invent innovative solutions that never existed before is the only way to find enduring solutions to complex problems – the kind of solutions that stick.

As we touched on earlier, there is ample evidence to suggest that many of the major social problems we now face qualify as complex dilemmas. We become paralysed in the face of the unsolvable. Today's tendency to simplify problems and seek quick fixes only increases the challenge. We are actually starting to realise that current courses of action aren't working. Decision and policy-makers are struggling to come up with viable alternatives.

In 2011, psychologist and thinker Daniel Kahneman published a new book called *"Thinking Fast and Slow"* which identifies two distinct systems that drive the way we think. System One is fast, intuitive and emotional; it operates automatically and quickly, with little or no effort and no sense of voluntary control while generating surprisingly complex patterns of ideas. System One thinking allows us to detect distances, to turn towards the source of a sudden sound, to complete a familiar phrase or saying, to 'read' body language and detect hostility in a voice automatically requiring little or no effort.

System Two is slower, more deliberative and more logical; it requires hard mental activities that include concentration, learning and judgement because it constructs thoughts in an orderly series of steps. System Two thinking requires attention and is disrupted when attention is drawn away. It allows us to add up a list of figures, search memory to identify a surprising sound, fill out a form or check the validity of a complex logical argument.

Together, Systems One and Two shape our impressions of our world and help us make decisions of all kinds. The issue Dr Kahneman focuses on is the tendency for people in contemporary societies to rely on intuitive, fast-response System One thinking, even when exploring dilemmas and finding solutions to complex and controversial problems.

Traditionally, it's been widely accepted by political leaders, senior bureaucrats, project managers and corporate leaders that the public is only capable of reacting and protesting. At the same time, stakeholders have held the view that governments and decision-makers aren't really interested in telling them the whole story or encouraging them to be a part of the solution. They believe that leaders treat them like children, occupy a paternalistic air, and have low expectations of the community as a whole. As a result, scepticism and cynicism have reigned supreme.

It is our contention that such dilemmas as the refugee question, the obesity problem, the climate change problem, even the drug and alcohol problem, will need collaboration between many stakeholders to identify potential actions as well as implementation activities. These collaborations need to be exploratory learning exercises where groups of people work together using Dr Kahneman's careful and considered System Two thinking. Such collaborative practice requires a flexible approach, ongoing monitoring and a willingness to change the approach based on feedback and new knowledge.

The need for something new

Throughout our 25 year involvement with both stakeholders and decision-makers, the art and science of community consultation is something that has undergone a profound evolution. Traditionally, a process would have commenced when a government agency or organisation had already made a decision that was going to affect its stakeholders. Only then would they seek input or comments from those who were due to be impacted. The subtext was, essentially, *"This is what we're going to do - tell us if you don't like it."*

Consequently, communities were required to comment on proposals or plans without any real knowledge or understanding of why that particular decision had been made in the first place or what problem it was intended to solve. Their responses were a matter of individual opinion, perhaps a result of Dr Kahneman's System One thinking.

Far from ideal, this approach (which often generated disagreement, argument and confrontation) understandably gave rise to feelings of anger, mistrust, disenchantment and disempowerment within the communities consulted.

However, had stakeholders been granted access to the bigger picture during all stages of the process of problem solving, rather than simply being sold a solution that had already been decided upon, the resulting conversation could have been very different.

So instead, when faced with complex dilemmas, an approach is needed that can provide a compelling incentive for politicians and decision-makers within government and corporate bureaucracies to explore those dilemmas with stakeholders.

This means approaching complex social problems differently. A commitment from decision-makers and stakeholders to work collaboratively and develop a shared definition of the dilemma is required before any attempt is made to find sustainable, enduring solutions.

Decision-makers, through more positive experiences, need to become confident in the capability of the populace to comprehend complexity and collaborate to find solutions that will stick.

Collaborative processes have far more potential for success than traditional consultation models.

We have spent time reviewing what others say about collaboration.

Collaboration is *"…the pooling of appreciations and/or tangible resources, e.g. information, money, labour, etc., by two or more stakeholders to solve a set of problems which neither can solve individually."* (Gray 1985)

*"**Collaboration** is the process of shared creation; two or more individuals with complementary skills interacting to create a shared understanding that none had previously possessed or could have come to on their own. Collaboration creates a shared meaning about a process ... Something is*

there that wasn't there before." (Michael Schrage 1990)

*"Issues for which a **collaborative** process will be useful are likely to be complex, requiring enduring solutions and involving multiple stakeholders."* (Alastair Bisley 2011)

*"Innovation is about divergent thinking and the creation of something new, and **collaboration** is an essential tool for achieving it. Like all creative forces, it is messy and unpredictable. Unlike cooperation, coordination, and communication it is not a planned exercise or a tidy ten-step process. This C word is different!"* (Leo Denise, The Rensselaerville Institute 2010)

Collaborations... *"are highly vulnerable to the protocols required by larger forms of togetherness. They do not fare well under ground rules -whether of agendas, turn taking, or almost anything else. Collaborations are interpersonally rather than structurally determined."* (Leo Denise, The Rensselaerville Institute 2010

The promise to **collaborators**...*"We will look to you for direct advice and innovation in formulating solutions and incorporate your advice and recommendations in to decisions to the maximum extent possible."* (International Association for Public Participation 2002)

*"**Collaborative governance** is a way of working with diverse stakeholders to create enduring solutions to our most complex issues, problems and dilemmas."* Twyfords 2011

From our research and experience working with clients and stakeholders over 20-plus years we believe that collaborative practice represents the best way forward for societies when it comes approaching and exploring its pressing problems and dilemmas. Using our own Appreciative Inquiry process we explored our most positive experiences of engaging with communities on challenging projects.

From those conversations we drew the five essential elements of good practice that have provided the greatest benefits to clients and stakeholders. We think those are:- appreciative mindsets; shared learning; trustful relationships; sophisticated conversations and thoughtful deliberation. From this work we have developed our Collaborative Governance model, now the focus of our work and the heart of our company.

Collaborative Governance

In this book we present our experiences of where ordinary people have been invited into the dilemma and, given the opportunity to contribute, have formulated rich and lasting outcomes.

We are promoting a system of thinking and a collaborative framework that supports the exploration of complex issues more deeply. We have called it "Collaborative Governance" because it is about collaborative decision-making.

One client, when presented with the model, called it a 'hope machine' because it gives stakeholders hope for a solution at the end of a journey together.

This book is our first attempt to describe the model and discuss our experiences of projects where we watched our client organisations and their communities demonstrate effective collaborative practice in both micro and macro situations.

Over the past 20 years we've encouraged decision-makers to have a different kind of conversation with their stakeholders, including their constituents and the people who have an opinion or who may be affected. Our clients now talk to a wide range of parties about a problem and the evidence that supports a need for action. The parties have started working together to create solutions. While it's been a challenging approach for many, it's our contention that when people are invited in to help understand and appreciate a particular problem and given the responsibility to step into a place where they can start to build solutions, they are able to rise to the occasion and surpass all expectations.

FIG. 2 – TWYFORDS' COLLABORATIVE GOVERNANCE MODEL

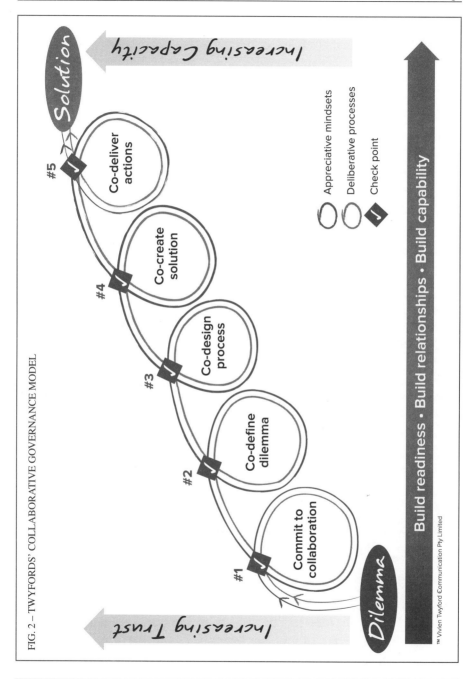

TM Vivien Twyford Communication Pty Limited

Why now?

The need to address complex problems using a collaborative problem-solving model is a greater necessity now than ever before. Why? Quite simply, the enormity of the challenges currently posed to us all by complex problems at this particular juncture in history is unprecedented. Indeed, many of the complex issues we face today simply didn't qualify as major challenges 30, 20 or even 10 years ago. Many didn't even exist.

The issues we've already mentioned like climate change (itself more complex than any phenomenon we've had to contend with before), atmospheric pollution, terrorism, asylum seekers, childhood obesity, adult obesity, natural resource scarcity, food shortages and developments needed to accommodate ever-increasing population levels, represent the type of contemporary issues that involve many competing interests and seem to defy solution.

Urgency also arises from the realisation that current approaches are simply not working. Paradoxically, as the challenges of complex issues become more pressing and dire, factors like compassion fatigue reduce our desire to understand or respond. We see so many problems and none of them appear any closer to being solved so we actually stick our heads in the sand and say, "this is all too hard".

Compounding the situation are things like e-mail campaigns by extremely worthy organisations that constantly appeal to our conscience and better natures, requesting us to sign up for or donate to a never-ending string of vital causes or initiatives. In the end, we push it all aside, unable to deal with the constant reminder of highly distressing problems and the fact that not too many of them are being solved in a sustainable way.

For business and corporations, the need to possess a social license to operate also heightens the need to comprehensively address the complex. Today, businesses have to function in a more complex, politically charged, culturally-aware social setting than they once used to. Gone are the days where a company CEO can decide to build a dam or coal mine whenever he or she wants to. Now, they need to acquire a high degree of social acceptance and must therefore be prepared to work with stakeholders. Like it or not, the community has the knowledge and can exercise the power of veto on a whim.

There are a number of factors that have contributed to this radical shift.

Firstly, there's the fact that people have learned how to use the system. That is, they know how to get in front of politicians and make their feelings heard.

Then there are the demands of demographics such as Generation Y. Masters of social media manipulation, they're more connected, engaged and prone to sharing information than any generation before. Though cynicism and scepticism remains a cornerstone of their mindsets, they want to dig deeper, expose hidden truths, and get behind important issues.

They understand the simplified superficiality of political agendas and associated media coverage and have become more interrogating as a result. They are demanding something better.

As we've discussed already, the role of the media in helping to generate this current state of play is also a factor in the need for the embracing of collaborative problem solving models. The bottom lines of news organisations everywhere have been suffering due to technological innovations and changing consumer habits. As a result, the negative, adversarial stories routinely generated by complex problems are viewed by media executives as vital to maintaining readership and market share.

However, on a more positive note, the same technological innovations that have reduced traditional media profits have also provided new forums for qualitatively different conversations. Social media tools like Facebook and Twitter provide opportunities for decision-makers to engage with a much bigger audience quickly and inexpensively. Communication, coordination and cooperation can be achieved outside the adversarial culture of the media.

A compelling need for developing positive relationships and trust

A lack of trust in political institutions also affects political decision-makers' ability to work with their communities. During the past two or three decades we have seen an increase in cynicism around governments and the governed. Communities are no longer satisfied to leave all the decisions to their elected representatives because they no longer trust them to look after their interests.

However, on the flip side, some elected representatives are equally frustrated about how they are expected merely to rubber stamp decisions made by appointed executives or bureaucrats. A similar frustration exists regarding the behaviour of multi-national corporations and big business.

Media coverage, highlighting the lack of ethics and values exhibited by many large organisations, depicts them as entities mostly concerned with profit, prepared to pay huge salaries and bonuses to executives while cutting jobs, whittling away employee benefits and demonstrating little or no concern for customers and community.

The Occupy movement, an international protest initiative primarily directed against economic and social inequality, demonstrates the level of frustration with key aspects of democratic systems around the world.

In particular the movement's focus is on the ability of the big end of town to influence political decision-making. While goals of the movement are not always clear, equal distribution of income, more and better jobs, bank and financial reform and a reduction of the influence of corporations on politics appear to be its main demands.

It's the fundamental lack of trust between communities and government, corporations and even non-government organisations that often frustrate attempts at complex problem solving.

Additionally, modern governments are defined by short political cycles. Consequently, it's not easy or even possible to come up with robust policy responses to profound or chronic dilemmas when politicians and voters are conditioned only to think about the next two or three years and seek an initial 'quick fix' that will look good and satisfy voters.

Most of the dilemmas facing us today require a longer-term response which only governments at the beginning of their term with a solid parliamentary majority, clear policies and a mandate for action can start to address effectively.

For these reasons it is important for political parties, as well as multi-national corporations, to start regular dialogues with their stakeholders to build understanding, share experiences, listen to one another and develop trust.

The Power of 'Co' supports the exploration of individual and organisational strengths, good practice and success. Using an appreciative approach, the Magic of 'Co' supports exploration of a desired future and then ways of achieving it. Such an approach develops enthusiasm, trust and cooperation.

Asking a useful question

When our leaders expect poor participation or assume a poor ability to cope with complex dilemmas, then unfortunately that's what they tend to get. Sadly, this is the context in which much of our current decision-making takes place.

Therefore the strategy adopted by many decision-makers essentially becomes: *"Let's make it as simple as possible for these people to understand. Let's bring it down to bite-sized chunks of easily digestible information about the actions we propose to take rather than giving people the richness of the current dilemma and exploring creative ways of solving it."*

Stanford University professor James Fishkin once asked, *"What is it that people would support if they had access to good and balanced information, time to think about it, time to deliberate over it, and discuss it with their fellow citizens?"* It's a fascinating question to which we would also add: *"What would all of us think (leaders, stakeholders, communities and experts*

*alike) if we all shared an understanding of the full complexity of an issue
or dilemma? What would we then support? What would we then see as a
way forward?"*

Our experience leads us to believe that the quality of collaboration is often
determined by the questions asked of the collaborators. The traditional
"consultation" approach all too often sounds like: *"Here is some information,
tell us what you think,"* or even: *"Have your say about this issue"*, which
is not a good start for a genuine and meaningful conversation. However,
when you start by providing evidence of an emerging issue or problem and
then ask how stakeholders have experienced the issue and whether they
have a different perspective, two things happen.

Firstly, a genuine conversation ensues where people start to listen to one
another. Secondly, if the conversation is well facilitated and all input is
respected, trust and positive relationships start to develop. As a result a
shared picture of the dilemma emerges.

Looking back at the Auckland motorway example in the introduction,
when the question posed (not always overtly) was: *"Should we toll or not
toll?"* the result is often polarity – support versus opposition for a particular
solution. When the people of Auckland appreciated the complexity, the
key question then became: *"What's the best way we can get this asset built
as fairly and as quickly as possible?"* This episode reinforces the idea
that when people appreciate a dilemma more deeply, they are able to help
identify better ways forward. That often starts with asking a more strategic
and useful question.

Another illustration of the need to ask the right questions with a view to
making good decisions is a simple story about 10-year-old Angus. He
was preparing to leave for a school excursion one day when his mum said,
*"Angus, why don't you take your little bag with you today rather than
carrying your big school bag on an excursion? Your little bag is hanging
up down the hall."* Angus took the smaller bag, wondering all the time
why. At the end of the day Angus showed up at his father's workplace. *"I*

couldn't catch the bus because my bus pass is in my big bag," was Angus's explanation.

Angus's parents could perhaps have asked different questions before making the decision about which bag Angus should take. They might have taken a little more time to explore the problem. A question about the choice of bag that would allow Angus to enjoy the excursion and manage his other commitments might have helped Angus contribute his perspective. As it was, his parents narrowed the dilemma down to the size and weight of the bag and created another problem for Angus to solve.

Key Learnings from Chapter 1

- Societies today are dealing with issues that are qualitatively different, more complex and more difficult to understand than ever before.

- Our traditional problem-solving methods are more suitable for simple and complicated problems than complex dilemmas.

- Mass media and its audiences thrive on adversarial stories featuring simplistic diametrically opposed positions. When the dominant narrative is polarised, it is easy to step into ever-firmer positions than to explore complexity.

- There is an urgent need for a different approach to complex issues that builds positive relationships and trust between leaders and citizens.

- Asking insightful questions help open up the conversation to different perspectives.

Chapter 2

The Paradox of Power

"The most exquisite paradox... as soon as you give it all up, you can have it all. As long as you want power, you can't have it. The minute you don't want power, you'll have more than you ever dreamed possible."

Ram Dass

The Paradox Explained

We explained in our introduction that the exercise of power can create a paradox for the powerful. We suggested that there is a challenge for elected representatives, corporate directors, executives and others in authority in deciding how best to use the power that their positions grant them. This chapter explores this idea further.

Power, or the ability to influence others, manifests in many ways. Sociologists offer distinctions between different types of power, including:

- **Positional power** that comes from holding formal authority delegated by others.
- **Expert power** that comes from having skills or expertise desired by others.
- **Personal power** that comes from having personality and charisma admired by others.
- **Reward power** that comes from the ability to provide rewards valued by others.
- **Informational power** that comes from being able to use or give valuable information to others or withhold valuable information from others.
- **Coercive power** that comes from being able to punish or manipulate others by withholding desired rewards or applying physical force.

However, sociologists also suggest that the exercise of power requires the consent or compliance of others. Power cannot be taken unless others are prepared to give it in return for desired benefits or to avoid negative outcomes. This creates a paradox or apparent contradiction.

Even in the case of coercive power, where force is exerted in the form of threats of psychological or physical punishment (torture or death), the fact that there are victims who are prepared to endure physical pain or even die rather than accept the authority of others demonstrates that even single, apparently powerless individuals can deny another's power over them.

The positional power paradox

Looking around our modern democratic states it is clear that positional power has its limits in all of them. Those who govern countries, organisations or communities do so only with the consent of those governed via the relative constraints and limitations of governance frameworks. They exercise personal, expert, reward and informational power and have the ability to use coercive power in a range of situations only within legally defined boundaries and with permission.

Despite this, we tend to think of political power as the ultimate. Moreover, we think of those holding such power as seemingly invincible, possessing the inherent ability to do anything they have promised and the capacity to enable any decision they feel necessary. The way many of us see it, those in power follow their own path without being obliged to defer to anyone. But, to the chagrin of those who actually hold positions of power, they can often do much less than they thought because those who give them power also limit that power. This creates the paradox or contradiction of power.

History tells us that 10th century monarch Cnut (Canute) the Great had this rather humbling reality figured out a long time ago. Himself the son of a Viking king, he was fully aware of the illusory nature of his power. He knew he only had the power God and his people gave to him. Eager to demonstrate that he was nowhere near as powerful as his subjects made out, he organised a small demonstration. Twelfth century chronicler Henry of Huntingdon tells how Cnut set his throne by the seashore and commanded the tide to halt and not wet his feet and robes. Of course, just as we would expect, the tide continued to rise and washed over his feet and legs without respect to his royal person. According to the chronicles, the king leapt backwards, saying: *"Let all men know how empty and worthless is the power of kings, for there is none worthy of the name but he whom heaven, earth and sea obey by eternal laws."* History tells us that he never wore his crown again.

The story of Cnut has often been misinterpreted. He wasn't trying to prove his power over the waves and failing. He was demonstrating that even the power of kings was limited. In a nutshell, Cnut was seen as powerful because he'd had the power of a king bestowed upon him. As a man, he knew how limited his power was and wanted to demonstrate this to his courtiers.

This example from the ancient world neatly sums up the paradox or contradiction of power. ***Power cannot be taken. It can only be given. This means that the many who cede power to individuals are potentially as powerful as the few to whom it is granted.*** Modern day examples of the paradox abound.

Consider Ricardo Semler (from our introduction), who transformed a company by giving power to staff to make the types of decisions traditionally reserved for managers. As a result, he became more powerful, with his book *Maverick* becoming a powerful influence in the field of management theory throughout the 1990's.

From a political perspective, consider the situation for Australian Prime Minister Julia Gillard when her party led by only one seat in the Federal Parliament. When we consider that within a hung parliament just one politician can force through a policy or negotiate significant amendments based on a personal agenda, it's clear that even Prime Ministerial limitations are significant.

Similarly, when newly re-elected New Zealand Prime Minister John Key didn't quite get over the line in his National Party's own right in 2011, he had to collaborate with the elected members of minor parties to have any chance of implementing his election promises over his second three year term.

Consider also the power of a President of the United States of America.

The current elected and acknowledged leader of the free world, Barack Obama, is probably questioning the true extent of his power when it comes to implementing his promised health reforms or managing the country's trillion dollar debt crisis, he has continually struggled to get his policy reformations over the line. Indeed, the man dubbed the world's most powerful must at times feel powerless when he struggles to win sufficient support from both sides of politics.

The 2011 'Arab Spring' uprisings in the Middle East have also clearly illustrated the illusory nature of power, even within apparent dictatorships with no democratic governance. Both former Egyptian President Hosni Mubarak and former Tunisian President Zine El Abidine Ben Ali were leaders who, one evening, went to bed all-powerful, only to wake next day to find that their power was gone because their people were no longer willing to give it to them. Throughout much of 2011 we saw a similar situation unfold in Libya. While Colonel Muammar Gaddafi certainly controlled a fair portion of the country's firepower and had been using terror and armed force to subjugate his own people for decades, enough of his people made the decision not to accept his power any longer, no matter what it cost them personally, and eventually succeeded in ousting him as their leader.

As discussed in the previous chapter, over the past 20 or 30 years we have seen a dramatic change in the way the conversation between politicians and the media has been conducted. Three decades ago investigative journalists provided in-depth analyses of the issues of the day, formulating the big questions and recommending solutions from both sides of politics to largely discerning audiences.

Today the mass media has been fragmented by the advent of the Internet and the explosion in the number of available information sources. Investigative journalists are few and far between. Newspapers continue to reduce staff, focusing instead on maintaining advertising revenue to stay profitable. Television stations, meanwhile, opt to produce cheap "reality TV" at the expense of quality programming. All the while audiences increasingly choose to obtain their news and entertainment from an ever-expanding range of Internet sources.

In today's political arena, what matters is how popular you are and how popular you can make your policies. Political leaders don't seem to be following particular principles. They're just trying to get re-elected. They aim to influence their constituents' System One thinking so voters will effortlessly absorb impressions and feelings that will in turn influence their beliefs and choices. They make no attempt to engage their constituents' System Two thinking, to encourage voters to pay careful attention to the issues, learn about the dilemmas and take some responsibility for providing thoughtful input into finding solutions.

Making it ever more confusing for voters is also the fact that both sides of politics have moved to occupy the middle ground, thus abandoning their traditional and easily distinguishable positions of left and right. Now it's hard to tell the difference.

Consider also the multi-national organisations and large bureaucratic government departments whose leaders decide on major restructuring processes to increase organisational effectiveness or efficiency. The decision to restructure is taken and then announced along with reasons for the change and an outline of the objectives of the new structure. Employees without a place in the restructured organisation are either offered redundancy or their employment is simply terminated. Remaining personnel are told to get used to the realities of the new regime or leave.

When employees feel disenfranchised and powerless, their only visible or viable options for regaining a semblance of power are either to keep their heads down and keep doing what they always do while waiting for things to "come back to normal", or to actively undermine the new structure. Neither action helps restructuring arrangements bear fruit or achieve desired outcomes. In a similar way to politicians, business leaders who try to exercise positional power without permission find themselves with less power. This once again demonstrates the power paradox.

The expert power paradox

Expert power is exercised on the assumption that particular knowledge or expertise is both necessary and sufficient to solve social problems. However, addressing complexity in today's world and finding acceptable and implementable solutions includes making judgments based on values as well as known facts. When faced with complex dilemmas, technical expertise or scientific knowledge is rarely sufficient.

In Chapter One we used the Cynefin model to explain the distinction between complicated problems and complex ones. We have found this distinction useful when explaining 'the curse of the expert', or the expert power paradox. Experts are experts because of their knowledge, training and experience in a particular field or discipline. Water engineers are experts in pipes and pumps, civil engineers are experts in designing and constructing roads and bridges, architects are experts in building materials and building design, and accountants are experts in tracking, documenting, interpreting and recording the financial dealings of individuals and organisations. Such experts are very good at solving technical problems in their specialist field because they have relevant knowledge, skill and experience and can co-operate with other experts to find solutions to complicated problems.

However, as discussed by Leo Denise in his article published by the Rensselaerville Institute called *'Collaboration vs. C-Three (Cooperation, Coordination and Communication)'*, co-operation is not enough when solutions are required for complex problems. Co-operation is important as a way of exchanging information; however divergence is also important when solving complex dilemmas. Different ideas and different approaches are needed, perhaps as a challenge to the 'usual' way of doing things. If everyone brings only knowledge that they have gained in the past to solve a complex problem or dilemma, it is not likely to be enough. Finding solutions to complex dilemmas demands a desire to do things differently, to use information created by different ways of thinking to solve a new and challenging problem and to create something new. Complex dilemmas require interventions that are flexible, that are not afraid of trial and error or the admission of not knowing. Solving complex dilemmas requires collaborators to be open to learning something new from unexpected sources or outcomes.

We often hear the call for "best science" to be used in resolving controversial issues, such as those surrounding the competing water needs of irrigators, farmers and the environment in Eastern Australia's Murray Darling Basin. Or the question of whether fracking technology used for mining coal seam gas will damage aquifer water quality, thus inflicting serious unintended consequences on the environment. It is our view that these complex issues are fundamentally value dilemmas masquerading as scientific questions, and that attention to the science alone will never generate sufficient trust or agreement between the parties so that they can create implementable solutions together.

The 'curse of the expert' shows itself when self-appointed experts believe that people without specialist knowledge, skill and experience have nothing useful to contribute to the creation of an innovative and workable solution. They ignore or dismiss ideas from 'the mob', the 'swill from the pub', the 'great unwashed' – the types of labels we have heard used in patronising tones by experts to describe people without demonstrated qualifications who seek to be involved in decision-making processes around issues that affect them. This despite the fact that these people have researched widely and considered carefully because they care passionately.

The Power of 'Co' : the Smart Power option

What we call Smart Power, or the Power of 'Co', can be used by leaders to both recognise and overcome this paradox. It involves sharing power - inviting people to share dilemmas in order that they can also share the generation of solutions, and by owning them, take responsibility for implementing them and ensuring that they stick.

Smart Power is the choice to exercise power in a different way. It's acknowledgement by those in charge that there are definite limits to what they can achieve without shared thinking with others who are involved. It's the willingness to demonstrate an honest, transparent and collaborative approach to complex issues while admitting, King Cnut-style, to not having all the answers. Most importantly, it's about harnessing the collective wisdom of those who have a useful contribution to make. It's about harnessing all the available resources so that the ultimate decision can be informed, wise and enduring. Crucially, this does not equate to an abrogation of decision-making responsibility.

Smarter experts, effective politicians and stunning leaders use Smart Power or the Power of 'Co'. They learn to step into different kinds of solution-finding processes that provide them with more resources, more expertise, more creativity and more power to find innovative, acceptable, workable and enduring solutions.

Critical characteristics or qualities of leaders who exercise smart power include:

- a belief in the capacity of people – valuing the involvement of stakeholders with diverse perspectives as a critical component of building lasting solutions, and trusting that stakeholders can go beyond individual limitations and create more enduring solutions than leaders or experts alone ;
- a belief in the 'wisdom of crowds' – that enough people working together have the potential to create wise solutions;
- an appreciative focus - tapping into positive experiences of success and the strengths of individuals to create energy, enthusiasm, positive relationships with stakeholders and a collective trust in the process.
- curiosity – a genuine desire to learn from others to deepen a shared understanding of the scope of the dilemma (alongside an expectation that better understanding will lead to innovation);
- a willingness (or perhaps a determination) to work for as long as it takes, to reflect, engage in dialogue, and deliberate together to seek powerful judgments, so that enduring solutions can be found.

Believing in people involves a mindset that recognises people as an asset and engagement as an opportunity to understand a diverse range of existing perspectives. It involves valuing diversity above agreement. It encourages purposeful engagement with a view to finding those with a genuine interest in the dilemma and a perspective that could illuminate, develop the field of vision and support innovation. It seeks out stakeholders representing diverse perspectives as a source of wisdom, rather than opponents to manage, placate, or out-muscle.

The wisdom of crowds involves accepting a simple but powerful truth that groups of individuals are mostly smarter than the smartest people charged with ultimately making decisions. It involves understanding that a group's collective intelligence is not determined by its individual members' knowledge or skill; if the group is large enough, diverse enough and independent enough it can solve complex problems through creatively using tension, disagreement and competition.

The appreciative approach involves the examination and exploration of successes or times when we have been at our very best. Appreciative Inquiry is an approach to creating positive change and includes a significant body of research and applied techniques. The aim is to focus on what works, on the basis that what we focus on is what we get more of. The aim is to understand strengths and opportunities rather than trying to understand weaknesses that have prevented success in the past. Focusing on the positive creates individual and group energy to generate together the image of a possible desired future. Group members learn and acknowledge that all players seek an enduring solution, despite potentially different positions. Tapping into a collective vision, founded on their own collective best experiences, is a way of changing the game.

Curiosity involves a willingness to ask important insightful questions, to explore why others have different views or perspectives, to find others who have common interests, and to share ideas and possibilities. It is also about genuinely inquiring into the strengths possessed by all stakeholders. If these questions are never asked then the power of different perspectives is never understood. Those stakeholders will feel unvalued and wise contributions may be lost. As a result, the eventual solution may be less enduring.

Staying open to new ideas involves being prepared to spend time, energy and effort listening to and learning from others. It involves dialogue and conversation rather than argument and debate. Individuals open to new ideas will explore together all facets of a dilemma while developing positive relationships and trust before deliberating on and then agreeing to particular solutions. According to Dr Lyn Carson, such deliberation requires a transparently representative stakeholder group, working in a safe and moderated space, in the clear knowledge that their work will be valued and will contribute to the creation of potentially sustainable and enduring solutions.

Leadership and the Power of 'Co'
Leaders need to be open to the possibility of doing things differently. Smart Power involves a willingness - when faced with complex, controversial and challenging dilemmas - to try something new that circumvents the power paradox and opens the door to meaningful alternatives.

Committing to the use of Smart Power, then exploring the true nature of a problem through sharing stakeholder perspectives, are the first steps in using the Power of 'Co'.

The performance of Queensland Premier Anna Bligh in addressing a downturn in the State's building industry in early 2011 is a watershed example of a modern leader opting for such an approach. Premier Bligh brought together a broad range of stakeholders in the building industry at a Building Revitalisation Forum in Brisbane.

Her opening session was attended by individual and corporate developers, architects, builders, building suppliers, financiers, as well as local and state government representatives. In essence, she told them: *"The reason we're getting you all together is that we know we can't address this ourselves. State government alone cannot address it because we don't hold all the levers. We don't control the decisions that banks make about who they lend to. We can't control whether people choose to live in Queensland. We can't control local government planning processes. So, we actually need you in on this because, while we're all part of the problem we're also potentially part of the solution. We need to recognise that we all have a part to play."*

It was an important and innovative step. While the building industry and the wider electorate were typically reacting to the downturn with the demand that "they" (meaning government and elected officials) fix the problem and sort the industry out, the Queensland government didn't have access to a magic wand. When it came to revitalising the construction industry, the government didn't have a bucket of money that they could dip into to or a range of levers they could pull. It couldn't create a whole new batch of developments in order to use up existing unused building materials that were floating around southern Queensland. They didn't have control over the Federal Government's immigration policy nor whether people living in Victoria or New South Wales chose to move to Queensland. Premier Bligh's admission was refreshing, and in the current political climate, almost revolutionary. So was the decision to invite everyone in to help solve the problem. In effect, she opted to share the power with a view to solving a major challenge.

Interestingly, the building industry conference wasn't the only occasion on which she had opted to take a different approach. Her performance throughout the 2011 Queensland flood crisis also earned her respect. Her instinctive response to share every piece of information she was privy to while herself trying to comprehend the enormity of the dilemma she was facing brought everyone watching her into her challenge. We all understood the dilemma she was facing as a leader. We, as casual observers, stood in her shoes.

There's no question that sharing her power in this way made her more powerful – both politically and personally. By adopting an inclusive, sharing approach, she revealed the dilemma and her inability to solve it, but simultaneously demonstrated true leadership. She recognised that she couldn't solve the problem alone. It was too big for one person and needed a collaborative approach for any sustainable solution to be found. It was a defining moment in Australian political life.

On a smaller scale, we saw another example of the challenge of power-sharing in the Wingecarribee Shire Council case study that we related in the introductory pages to this book. At the start of that project there were definite concerns from local government leaders about the approach we were suggesting. The key issues we heard included: *"What if people come up with something ridiculous? Are we going to be captured by particular interests or people with a single issue? Am I going to look like I'm abrogating my leadership responsibility by taking this approach? Shouldn't I have all the answers? After all, this is what I was elected for."* For them, asking their community to share the dilemma they were facing was a risky, vulnerable space to step into. However, they agreed to take the plunge into the unknown. And rather than being seen as being weak or derelict in their duties, the opportunity for community members to be involved was both embraced and widely appreciated.

As we have discussed, a significant challenge to the exercising of smart power is that many leaders believe that sharing their power effectively reduces their ability to exercise it. They contend that making someone else powerful is a challenge to their own sovereignty. Also contributing to this negative mindset is the concept we discussed earlier as the paradox of expert power (or 'the curse of the expert') which includes the expert's belief that they have all the necessary knowledge, skill and experience to solve any problem. Their subtext is often, *"If only you knew what I know, you'd understand it and would agree with my solutions."* A different and more useful subtext might be, *"If I only knew what you know, I could create a more informed, wiser and more enduring solution."*

However, despite the obvious challenges, we argue strongly that good leadership is not about making all the decisions all the time and expecting them all to be approved and be subsequently proved right. Decisions made quickly and intuitively based on Dr Kahneman's System One autopilot are often seriously affected by subconscious intuition and biases. The really gutsy, strong leaders of today are the ones who appreciate complexity and are prepared to ask others to step into the dilemma with them so the dilemma can be understood and solutions found together. This requires significant shared effort to use System Two thinking, systematically working through known facts and perspectives, designing rational governance arrangements and then creatively exploring possible solutions. But this is difficult and takes great courage and patience. It requires a studied departure from our intellectual and organisational comfort zone – a place where important decision-making has long been the prerogative of those at the top of the pyramid, using data and recommendations from those below.

To exercise the Power of 'Co' requires a change in mindset of many of today's leaders. Leaders who believe they need to be strong, decisive and uncompromising, and who think that having no ready-made solution already prepared in their back pocket is an admission of unacceptable weakness, need help and support to try a different way, even when their way of making decisions isn't working.

In its February 2007 issue *Harvard Business Review* published an article called 'In Praise of the Incomplete Leader'. Authors Ancona, Malone, Orlikowski and Senge suggest that 'it is time to end the myth of the complete leader: the flawless person at the top who's got it all figured out'. They suggest that the sheer complexity and ambiguity of problems facing our world today is humbling and it is impossible for any one person to stay on top of both the knowledge and the skills they need to not only survive, but thrive.

Having worked with hundreds of struggling leaders, the authors have developed a model of distributed leadership which identifies a set of four capabilities: *sensemaking* – interpreting developments in their environment; *relating* – building trusting relationships; *visioning* – communicating a compelling vision of the future; and *inventing* – coming up with new ways of doing things. They suggest that rarely, if ever, will one person be equally skilled in all four domains and that leaders need to balance their skill sets by finding and working with others. All the four skills require a curious mind and a willingness to explore the perspectives of others. In particular the authors suggest that, while traditional images of leaders are people who don't seek counsel from anyone other than their trusted inner circle and don't assign much value to relating, today's leaders need to be able to build trusting relationships using the key skills of enquiry, advocacy and connection.

One of the challenges faced by elected representatives in addressing the paradox is that the electorate too seems on the surface to demand that its leaders provide quick solutions to every problem that presents itself. This reinforces politicians' desires to offer simple solutions, portray the illusion of power and credibility, and thus confirm themselves as individuals worthy of re-election.

This pattern of behaviour can present a significant barrier to change, with any attempt to exercise a degree of smart power having the potential to be seen as some kind of weakness.

This was apparent in the wake of Julia Gillard's proposed Citizens' Assembly on climate change. The idea of inviting 150 community members to help find lasting solutions to such a pressing challenge was quickly ridiculed in the media and provided political ammunition with which to attack and undermine both the Prime Minister and her climate change policies. The powerful and the powerless were (and are) inclined to reject an unusual or non-traditional way of resolving a problem or making a decision, no matter how doggedly the problem has resisted solution in the past. Sticking with the known, even when regularly unsuccessful, often appears safer than trying something different. We as a society colluded in that particular decision because we told her, in effect, that collaboration is not what an effective leader does.

The episode clearly demonstrates the challenge of different mindsets around leadership and decision-making. For many people in Australia, the Prime Minister is seen as someone with the responsibility to make and sell the tough decisions herself. When she talks about asking 150 people to help her achieve a particular outcome, she is seen as weak and abrogating her role as a leader. A leader doesn't confer with 150 faceless people about society's problems. A leader makes decisions.

However, not all people feel the same about how leaders make decisions. In many situations stakeholders and communities want to have a real say in decisions that affect them. They become angry and upset when 'consultation' appears to be token or merely an attempt to sell a decision already made.

When leaders take on the 'curse of the expert' using both positional and expert power to convince stakeholders that a particular decision (made non-transparently) is the right one and should be accepted, they often find that stakeholders or entire communities become angry and emotional. This is particularly the case when the outcomes of that decision will have negative consequences for them personally or for something that they value.

Community outrage is a common reaction to this kind of decision-making. If enough people are sufficiently opposed to or upset by the decisions of the powerful they can, and do, force decision-makers to reverse their decisions.

The outcome of such conflict and confrontation doesn't build positive relationships. Long memories can ensure that resentment boils for years and long-standing grievances about past decision-making practices can make long-term communication between the relevant parties difficult and sometimes quite toxic.

We recommend a more interesting and effective way to lead in the 21st century.

Developing partnerships and collaborating with others in data gathering and data interpretation will result in more robust sensemaking. Building trusting relationships by listening to and understanding the perspectives of others (inquiry) and clarifying specific observations, interpretations and judgements to others without aggression or defensiveness (advocacy) are the skills used by effective leaders in connecting and relating.

Walking the walk and embodying core values and ideas are all part of effective visioning. Inventing is what moves ideas and visions into the real world of implementation. "If I keep on doing what I've always done, I'll keep on getting what I've always got!" is an expression we are all familiar with. Innovative outcomes require creativity; collaborative practice helps people figure out new ways of working together.

Fundamentals of the Power of 'Co'
The Power of 'Co' or Smart Power reflects this kind of leadership. It includes recognising the limits to our positional and expert power and tapping into not only our own wisdom but also the wisdom of all those interested, energetic individuals who have a stake in the outcome of our actions.

Leadership success hinges on a shared appreciation of the context, the constraints, and the dimensions of situations or issues in order to recognise that we are not always in charge, and be able to surrender the need to control the process and the outcome. Leaders need to build positive and trustful relationships between those who can help find solutions. They need to support processes that allow robust solutions to emerge from careful deliberation.

Conversations lead us to relationships, which in turn lead us to transactions. It's a process that can't be circumvented. Conversations first build relationships. When trustful relationships exist, creative solutions become possible. Without trust there is unlikely to be creativity.

Smart leadership is not about holding onto power. It's not about coming up with all the answers. Smart leadership is about recognising limits to power and drawing on the collective knowledge and wisdom of others.

In our work, we have seen leaders achieve more power when they let go and accepted help from diverse sources that enabled them to arrive at solutions that would have been otherwise unattainable. We've seen them experience the realisation that this is a stronger and wiser way to lead.

Demonstrating the Fundamentals
Here are some of our stories of where the Power of 'Co', or Smart Power,

has been exercised in a practical way to achieve success.

Believing in people

One small but notable example took place when we were doing some work with a local council, the bane of whose existence was a virulent activist who took every opportunity to denigrate council and its staff. We were warned that the activist was going to be our biggest problem. However, a conversation with this person at his home, while a simple act, had lasting consequences. While the activist continued to disagree with everything we and our client did, the relationship we built allowed ongoing conversations. Rather than demonise the person in question, we chose to see him as an individual who was interested and passionate about community affairs. Building this relationship was a critical part of the eventual success of the project.

Believing in the wisdom of crowds

In 2001 we were involved in a land use planning project on the edge of San Diego in the USA. It entailed a complex dilemma involving the competing interests of farmers, agriculturalists, environmentalists, developers, and people looking for affordable housing. No matter what proposals were floated, local authorities were getting pilloried constantly by one interest group or another and quickly became stuck. On the advice of a colleague of ours, the Mayor agreed to try a totally different approach.

This involved the Mayor bringing all the different interest groups together and telling them that if they could come up with a solution they could all live with, he would support it. While the approach could have seen the Mayor accused of abrogating responsibility, he chose to sell the strategy as a means of exercising his responsibility. He also recognised that giving other people the power actually made him more powerful because he was more likely to achieve an outcome that would really deliver.

At the outset, he acknowledged all the challenges, issues and legitimate interests and concerns in play, and highlighted the challenge for the interest groups of working together. He recommended that the groups engage in conversations so they understood each other's perspectives and views before co-creating a solution that was fair, reasonable and sustainable. The approach worked. After a few days the participating parties came up with something they could all accept. As a result of the power sharing strategy, most agricultural land and areas of environmental importance were preserved, while those people whose land was being bought up were appropriately compensated.

The appreciative approach

Arguably the most revered political and ideological leader of his generation, Mahatma Gandhi was a figure who was prepared to demonstrate his vulnerability and weakness. In doing so, he found he had unprecedented power and influence.

Following the establishment of Indian independence in 1947, Gandhi faced a complex problem. It had been decided that India (at that time home to Hindus and Muslims who found it difficult to live together peacefully) would be partitioned into two separate countries. The central part of India was to remain essentially a Hindu country, while the new country of Pakistan became Muslim. This meant a mass migration of both Hindus and Muslims. Hindus who lived in what was to become Pakistan moved to Hindu India. Muslims living in the part of India remaining Hindu moved to either East or West Pakistan.

The level of excitement and fear in the Punjab region generated by the migration of millions of people created vast social unrest leading to violence and slaughter despite the best efforts of the army to manage the situation.

In the eastern city of Calcutta the situation was predicted to become even more catastrophic. With the army unable to maintain a presence in both locations, Gandhi, a Hindu leader, offered to go there himself. His strategy for quelling the unrest was to live in a house with the local Muslim leader without any security or protection – an approach deemed by many as virtually suicidal. By doing so he was able to forge an atmosphere of togetherness and common humanity within the host community. When partition was complete and a huge planned celebration called Freedom at Midnight commenced, thousands of people, both Hindu and Muslim, danced and sang in the streets of Calcutta.

Thanks to his belief that people could co-exist and his willingness to embrace his powerlessness and vulnerability, Gandhi was able to closely interact with those who were viewed by others as highly adversarial, and achieve an outcome previously thought impossible. Gandhi, who famously said, *"Let's actually think about what is it that people are doing right when they are able to achieve such great things"*, created a remarkable phenomenon single-handedly. He chose to believe in the best in people and created a surprising outcome.

Curiosity and staying open to new ideas

Several years ago, the local council of the small NSW coastal town of Kiama was under pressure to either allow for the continued propagation of urban sprawl or opt for a strategy of medium to high-density housing in an attempt to accommodate population growth. When they settled on the medium density option and sought community approval for their decision via a survey, the response was entirely negative. In essence, the community had been presented with Council's solution to a problem that they themselves had defined.

Certainly, the alternative urban sprawl was also a problematic outcome, especially considering the potential for distinct local townships such as Gerringong, Gerroa and Jamberoo to join up as housing growth intensified. Therefore, the question of how to manage population growth was certainly another dilemma that needed urgent attention. However, Council's question to the community regarding the issue wasn't terribly creative. It was, effectively, 'Is it OK if we intensify development?' It was an approach that failed to generate any form of community consensus or workable solution and the decision was shelved.

Two years later we were involved in a very different type of process. While the initial strategy had involved the Council imposing a decision, the

Councillors this time decided, reluctantly at first, to give up some of their power. They were curious about the reasons why the Kiama community had so roundly rejected their previous planning solution and wanted to understand the different values held about living in the area. The dilemma of population expansion and future development of Kiama hadn't gone away. They decided to use a more deliberative approach and engage with community members, State government agencies, developers and farmers before commissioning a citizens' jury to provide recommendations. In the course of the many stakeholder conversations that were initiated, a multitude of differing perspectives and realities emerged. These included concerns regarding the pressure on agricultural land, the desire of many locals to preserve the integrity of the rolling green hills around Kiama, and the desire to preserve the character of distinct townships.

There was also recognition that Kiama sits within the State of New South Wales and that the State Government was committed to its own growth targets. In short, zero population growth was not an option and people accepted that. When they also recognised and appreciated that the area constituted a fairly rare pocket of productive coastal land that benefited from relatively high rainfall levels, they approached the problem quite differently and put forward a better question.

This time, that all-important question that was put to the citizens' jury took the form of: *"What is the best way for Kiama to accommodate population growth whilst retaining the character of the town, maintaining the valued scenery, retaining agricultural land and maintaining the distinct townships?"* This led planners to explore a number of vacant lots as well as draw on exciting new designs for duplex developments. In the end, the emerging citizens' consensus was that careful medium-density development would be a much better way of accommodating population growth and preventing the damaging effects of urban sprawl.

Consensus was achievable because all relevant parties were involved in defining and understanding the challenges that faced the local area. A randomly selected group of local citizens was charged with learning, deliberating and arriving at a solution they all agreed with. This time around, the problem and solution were not pre-defined by Council planners and Councillors and thus no energy had to be expended on selling or defending the decision to a suspicious community. The deliberative approach allowed the jury and those witnesses who provided evidence to the jury members to think about things differently. While the idea of multiple duplex or villa developments springing up all over the countryside previously initiated howls of protest, an in-depth appreciation of the pervading realities enabled the jurors to operate within a different framework. As a result, the response was more like, "This is OK - we can cope with this because we know it will maintain the identity of our township."

In the end, Council effectively let go of their power to make this decision while holding on to their responsibility to ensure a wise decision was made. If they had tried to impose an unpopular high-rise solution they would have struggled to get their legislation through, thus becoming less powerful as a result. But by opting for Smart Power and exercising it in a different way, they facilitated higher quality outcomes that delivered something for everybody – Councillors, community and stakeholders alike.

These then are the fundamentals of Smart Power, or as we call it, the Power of 'Co'. Believing in people and their ability to solve problems together, believing in the value of diversity and the wisdom gained from understanding many perspectives, using the appreciative approach to tap into positive experiences of success and develop shared trust in a collaborative process, being curious about the range of interests, views and passions and finally, and perhaps most importantly, a willingness to take time and space to deliberate together to find solutions that stick.

Key Learnings from Chapter 2

- There are many forms of power. Smart leaders know when to share and distribute power.

- Collaboration fosters innovation through diversity and creative tension.

- When solving complex problems, leaders only have as much power as the "community of interest" is willing to give them.

- Letting go doesn't mean losing control.

- When facing complex dilemmas, we need to go beyond co-operation to collaboration to co-create enduring solutions.

- Command and control approaches to controversial issues are unlikely to generate solutions that stick.

Chapter 3

The Logic of Collaborative Decision-Making

"We are all gifted. That is our inheritance."

Ethel Waters

In 1989 Stephen Covey wrote an influential book called the *Seven Habits of Highly Effective People* in which he suggested that effectiveness is achieved through the application of seven particular principles and patterns of behaviour that support individual progress from dependence to interdependence and thence to effectiveness. All seven habits are important to achieve these ends but the discipline of his second habit, *Begin with the End in Mind*, is highly relevant to our backwards logic of Collaborative Governance. He suggests that *"To begin with the end in mind means to start with a clear understanding of your destination. It means to know where you're going so you better understand where you are now so that the steps you take are always in the right direction."*

This habit strikes us as being the essence of good planning. However, it is quite difficult to do well. In our experience it takes imagination, creativity, discipline and hard mental effort to clarify both what a desired future might look like and how you could test whether it had been achieved, even from one's own perspective. To try and work this out and get agreement from a range of others is even more challenging. Despite the difficulties, Covey's discipline of 'beginning with the end in mind' has helped us think through a reverse or backwards logic when describing our model of Collaborative Governance.

We believe that the Collaborative Governance model is logical. Each step in the process is an essential precursor to the step that follows. Step Two won't be successful unless Step One successfully precedes it. Step Three won't work without a successful conclusion of Steps One and Two. Most importantly, Step Four (dealing with the co-creation of enduring solutions through exploration of options, evaluation and deliberation) is unlikely to achieve stakeholder agreement on solutions without the outcomes of Steps One, Two and Three. We need the relationships and trust that arise from a shared understanding of not only what the dilemma entails, but also of the issues that are important to all parties when it comes to the solution and the process of achieving it.

This doesn't mean that there has to be a straight line relationship between Step One and Step Five. Collaborative Governance is about working with people and people don't necessarily think or progress logically in straight lines. We recognise that progress through the steps is likely to be iterative, messy and sometimes even tortuous. Some individuals and groups may need to revisit and renegotiate previous steps before being able to move forward in a later step and, however reluctantly, we may need to accept this.

However, we believe that, as one of our clients described it, the model can be seen as a road map that highlights a path from "stuckness" to "forward movement" - a means of turning a potentially unsolvable problem into an enduring solution. As such, it is a process more likely to achieve desired outcomes than most others available to us.

What follows is our reverse or backwards logic for the five steps that we describe in more detail in the next five chapters – beginning with the end in mind.

The end in mind for Collaborative Governance is *"Co-creation by diverse stakeholders through an informative, appreciative and deliberative process of enduring solutions to society's most complex issues"*.

Wikipedia in 2011 defines collaborative governance as *"... a process and a form of governance in which participants (parties, agencies, stakeholders) representing different interests are collectively empowered to make a policy decision or make recommendations to a final decision-maker who will not substantially change consensus recommendations from the group."*

At first look, then, it would seem that co-creating enduring solutions is the end point; the outcome of a deliberative solution-finding process than ends in consensus and is approved by the ultimate decision-maker.

However, in our view, the end point comes one step later, arriving after any agreement to or approval of a solution. We believe that to fulfill the meaning of "enduring" in relation to the solution, the solution first has to be implemented and, through implementation, demonstrate that it does indeed solve the problem and does not lead to the types of unintended consequences we described in Chapter One.

When we start to collaborate, we start to build the essential foundations required for successful implementation and delivery of the solutions we will create together. This is why our model of Collaborative Governance has five distinct and logical steps, with the end step, crucially, centering on a shared preparation for the effective delivery of the solution with input, energy and enthusiasm from all stakeholders who were part of the collaboration.

Our diagram shows that the desired outcome or end point of Collaborative Governance is about more than agreeing to a solution to a complex problem. It requires action to achieve the desired outcomes. How many strategies and plans have been created in the past only to sit on shelves because there is neither political will nor practical energy available to implement them? How many decisions have been made with so many compromises or trade-offs along the way that no stakeholder is willing to own them?

Implementation requires commitment to the solution as well as energy and support for the actions required to deliver it, to make it happen. Commitment, energy and action for implementation stems from ownership of the solution and a determination to see it put into practice. In order to achieve this endpoint of commitment, energy and action, there is a clear backwards logic through the five steps to our starting point.

We have suggested in Chapters One and Two that the Power of 'Co' is a paradox or contradiction. When faced with a complex or controversial problem or dilemma, leaders achieve more power by restricting their use of positional or expert power to control an outcome. Instead, when faced with a situation which is stuck as a result of disagreement, argument, emotion

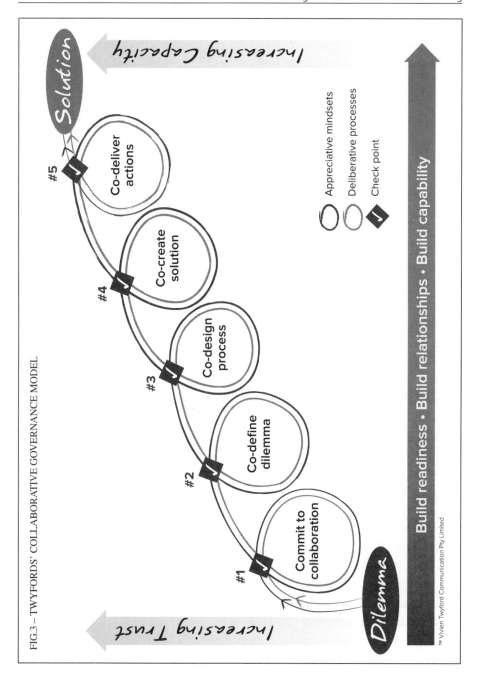

FIG.3 – TWYFORDS' COLLABORATIVE GOVERNANCE MODEL

Solution

Increasing Capacity

Increasing Trust

#5 — Co-deliver actions

#4 — Co-create solution

#3 — Co-design process

#2 — Co-define dilemma

#1 — Commit to collaboration

Dilemma

Appreciative mindsets

Deliberative processes

Check point

Build readiness • Build relationships • Build capability

™ Vivien Twyford Communication Pty Limited

and confrontation, we contend that leaders will get a better outcome if they invite the warring factions to step into the dilemma and work together to build trust, a shared understanding of the dilemma, as well as a process for actually working together.

Hopefully we have made it clear in earlier chapters that the Power of 'Co' does not mean that elected or appointed decision-makers abrogate their responsibility to find wise and enduring solutions to complex and potentially controversial dilemmas. Rather, this power means that leaders take greater responsibility for the problem-solving process - a process that will include all the 'co' words like commitment, cooperation, co-design, coordination, collaboration, communication, co-creation, and even coefficient (defined as having a multiplier effect that results in a superior outcome).

Since calling our model Collaborative Governance in early 2011, we have realised that this term was already in circulation and has increasingly been appearing in journal articles, publications and books. Leaders are looking for new approaches, as the problems they face are becoming more complex and their traditional problem solving methods aren't working.

However, in our model, Collaborative Governance is not just about finding solutions that stick. It's about a process that begins with the end in mind. It's about the development of positive relationships between the collaborators. It's about building resilience and trust among the collaborators and in the collaborative process as well as a commitment to continue working together until a solution is found and implemented.

There is a clear logic to the process that demonstrates that each step has its role in bringing diverse groups of stakeholders together to build the trust that supports the co-creation of enduring solutions.

F. For a solution to be enduring, stakeholders need to have a role in solution implementation

Our many years of experience in working with clients who genuinely want to engage communities in decision-making leads us to realise that trust and

FIG. 4 – TWYFORDS' BACKWARDS LOGIC MODEL

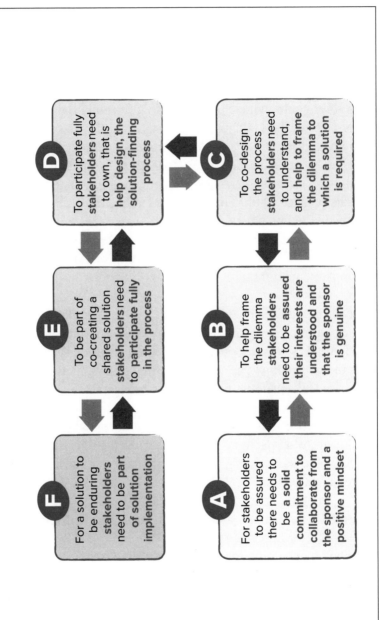

D To participate fully stakeholders need to own, that is help design, the solution-finding process

C To co-design the process stakeholders need to understand, and help to frame the dilemma to which a solution is required

E To be part of co-creating a shared solution stakeholders need to participate fully in the process

B To help frame the dilemma stakeholders need to be assured their interests are understood and that the sponsor is genuine

F For a solution to be enduring stakeholders need to be part of solution implementation

A For stakeholders to be assured there needs to be a solid commitment to collaborate from the sponsor and a positive mindset

a sense of ownership among those contributing to a particular solution is paramount for the achievement of sustainable and supported outcomes. In other words, for a solution to be enduring, stakeholders need to have sufficient interest and energy to assume a role in its implementation.

Such roles could include, for example: informing the wider community of interest about the collaborative process and the stakeholders involved in it; sharing information on the dilemma as defined by the group and the governance structure they defined together; explaining the shared solution and the plan for implementation; volunteering for a role in the implementation plan; helping to establish measures and indicators of success with those who will be on the implementation team; being advocates and spokespeople for the solution and its implementation with government, industry, community groups or NGOs; being part of the ongoing monitoring and evaluation of the implementation activities.

Once we recognise how important it is for stakeholders to have a high level of interest and energy in ensuring successful implementation of a shared solution, the key question then becomes: what does it take for sufficient trust and ownership to be achieved so that stakeholders will have the energy and interest in ensuring the solution is implemented appropriately?

Our experience tells us that in order for each stakeholder to be prepared to sign up to a specific role in delivering the agreed solution, Step Five must involve stakeholders determining the governance structure around the implementation.

This may entail deciding such things as: Who will manage the project? Who will be responsible for the resources needed? Who will oversight the implementation process? What will the roles, responsibilities and accountabilities be for each stakeholder? and, Who will be responsible for monitoring and evaluation?

For a solution to be enduring, each stakeholder needs to sign up to their role in delivering the agreed solution.

Example from our personal experience –

Taking the initiative in a Citizens' Panel in Wellington

In 2008 we saw a demonstration of real ownership by a group of people during a Citizens' Panel to support the development of Council's Long-Term Community Plan in Wellington, New Zealand. The Panel had 45 selected members whose job was to review Council's long-term planning process and make suggestions for improvements to the plan. Panel members attended several meetings where they reviewed the draft plan and then worked together to prioritise their issues and provide ideas and recommendations to Council.

At the penultimate panel meeting, panel members decided that they didn't want a Council staff member to write a report on recommendations they themselves had co-created. Instead, they wanted to compile it themselves. Panel members realised how hard it would be, in such a short time, to produce a report that all panel members could agree on. Instead, six panel members volunteered. They owned the recommendations they had co-created and wanted to make sure they were reported and presented accurately. These six individuals felt strongly enough about the importance of the report to go that extra mile. They stepped up and put in the effort needed to write a report and present a detailed, accurate and truthful representation of wider community sentiment. This influenced councillors to treat the contribution of the panel more seriously.

E. To be part of co-creating a shared solution, stakeholders need to participate fully in the process

For stakeholders, partners and contributors to have that crucial sense of ownership, they need to be involved in co-creating that solution. To co-create the solution they will need to share an understanding of the challenges they observed throughout the process, the different agendas among the collaborators, the passions and the emotions that surfaced, the options put forward, the conversations, the dialogue, even the tough hard-nosed negotiations as the solution took shape. When people have shared such an experience they will relate very differently to the decisions and actions that result from that process. That's because they can actually see their fingerprints all over the end result.

Conversely, in situations where stakeholders are asked to accept a solution created by someone else without knowing the processes by which it was generated, the combative and adversarial environment that often results tends to undermine even an apparently technically or scientifically valid solution. Indeed, we've learned that there can be a lot of mistrust if people feel like a consultation process has been done to them and that they're being socially engineered to achieve the outcome that a sponsor wants.

Being part of the solution-making process, in our view, means participating in processes that provide enough time and space for all collaborators to become well-informed - both about the objective facts of the dilemma and related issues and about the subjective perspectives and agendas of their co-collaborators and relevant stakeholders.

It is only in an environment of patience, empathy and understanding, with time to think and talk together using System Two thinking, dreaming of what might be, exploring options and evaluating impacts with people they trust, and then together co-creating shared solutions, that a group of collaborators is likely to achieve agreement.

To co-deliver actions, there must be a consensus on a solution.

Examples from our personal experience –

Port Phillip 21st Century Town Meeting

In 2008 Melbourne's Port Phillip Council ran a large deliberative community forum involving 800 people. Participants were being asked to help Council make important decisions about their services and activities so that Council's planning could better reflect community needs. Each participant had been provided with a booklet that explained the dilemma faced by Council, the specific decisions that Council had to make, background information and specific questions that Council sought answers to. As well as having conversations to better understand the context and then voting for particular options using hand-held technology, the participants could raise their own aspirations, ideas and concerns that were typed into a computer on their table.

These ideas were transmitted to a 'theme team' who consolidated them and presented the results regularly throughout the day on big screens.

Participants were fascinated to see their priorities and their ideas being acknowledged, validated and documented in full view of everyone. People were seeing themselves operating within the process and seeing their fingerprints on the screen in real-time.

Ground Zero collaboration

A similar model was used by America Speaks when they designed the collaborative framework for the rejuvenation of New York's Ground Zero after the destruction of the World Trade Centre in 2001.

The process, involving 4,500 New Yorkers, entailed participants being able to see a near-instant visual representation of their ideas and contributions.

When people take part in an assembly like this one, they share the different perspectives. They see that their viewpoint is one of many. Having the opportunity to learn what others have to say (inquiry) and to clearly voice their own opinion (advocacy) is extremely important, as it's this that establishes a vital sense of ownership. Importantly, this dynamic plays out within a large gathering of 4,500 people or a small group of 45.

D. To participate fully, stakeholders need to own (that is, help design) the solution-finding process

We can feel confident that stakeholders will be willing to co-create a problem-solving process if they believe their individual and collective needs have been understood and that the process they'll be using will ultimately address the co-defined problem parameters.

They need to know the recognised decision-making body that has the mandate to address the dilemma and to know this body has a commitment to the collaboration and won't allow it to be subverted. They also need to believe that this organisation acknowledges and values their contribution. To arrive at this point takes conversation, listening, empathy. Stakeholders need to share their own stories of how enduring decisions have been made in different circumstances and draw out the key factors that made them successful. They need to know that there is sufficient resourcing for the collaborative process and that enough time has been allocated for its implementation.

They must believe that they have an unconstrained responsibility to reach agreement on a solution to the problem. When they feel confident that the process is genuine and they are not being manipulated, they will be able to co-design a way of working together that's acceptable to all, including the ultimate decision-making body.

While some people may view the idea of stakeholders taking responsibility for process design as perilous, questioning how we might all work on a problem together is actually an incredibly practical thing to do.

Working together leads to clarity, as people gain confidence in each other and the group's ability to share ideas, conduct conversations and arrive at shared positions. Even if they don't have much influence on the governance structure, having an understanding of who the decision-makers are and the information they will base their decisions on builds confidence.

Brainstorming possible options for governance structures and collaborative processes within their specific context and available resources, then contributing to choosing the preferred one is most likely to achieve an agreed and workable design for the decision-making structure and governance process.

To be able to co-create solutions, there needs to be an agreed design for the decision-making structure and process.

Examples from our personal experience –

A successful co-design by NZTA

In 2011, The New Zealand Transport Agency (NZTA) was involved in implementing a collaborative framework that became a great example of co-design practice. Acting on a push from within the New Zealand central government (who was encouraging its agencies to put customers rather than departmental needs first), the agency opted to undertake some direct conversations with road users. The aim was to explore whether their services provided value for money. NZTA wanted to make sure they were both building the roads that New Zealand road users wanted and contributing to the long-term outcome of better national transport services.

Initially NZTA engineers were reluctant to participate. They had a tendency to see building technically superior roads as an end in itself and could see no benefit from sitting down to talk with customers in what they assumed would be some kind of group discussion.

Instead, they were given the opportunity to understand the dilemma faced by NZTA and co-design the process of talking to their road user customers. Despite initial reluctance, the group of engineers subsequently became champions of the initiative. They better understood road users' priorities, which made a huge difference when it came to implementing the change of policy direction.

A new approach in Gunnedah – a space to watch

Further challenges to co-creation and co-ownership can arise when people believe that somebody else has already designed the process in which they're being asked to participate. In Gunnedah, a town in northeastern New South Wales, the local farming community is at odds with various multinational proposals for coal seam gas drilling in their area. The anger and frustration of both parties has made it very difficult to get them working together. The gas companies believe they have a legal right to explore and resent the community's "shut the gate" reaction. The community, fearful of the impacts of mining exploration on farming properties, doesn't want to participate in a decision-making framework that feels as though it is intended to manipulate them. Having no say in the way they participate in the decision-making process, they feel railroaded and powerless and react angrily and aggressively. It's a situation amplified by a landscape dotted with many different views and polarised perspectives.

Our work to date has entailed encouraging the gas companies to create a process oversight group from within the Gunnedah community to scrutinise the proposals for mining exploration and then share the results of their analysis with the wider community. We have also talked to the community activists and shared the suggested approach with them. Both sides are cautious because trust is lacking and because their perspectives on the dilemma are so different. However, we believe that subjecting the mining exploration proposals to community scrutiny will serve to reduce angst, build relationships and change the nature of the conversation. Understanding the proposals, sharing information about the geology and environmental science, accepting what is not known and sharing in fact-finding activities means that both sides can share the responsibility for establishing whether risks to land and groundwater can be reduced enough for exploration to proceed.

In situations like this, it's far better to invite people in to design the process together before trying to create a solution collaboratively. Such an approach invites stakeholders into a safe place and results in a far less divisive conversation where complex issues are concerned. It's no secret that passionate people will prove virtually unstoppable when it comes to involving themselves in the content of an issue. The way forward is to tap into and accommodate that passion constructively using a different methodology. Indeed, a smart strategic question to get things unstuck could be, "How might we work together to make some progress on this issue?"

C. To co-design the process, stakeholders need to agree on the scope of the dilemma and what really matters in relation to its solution

This is the step during which it is critical to get all the relevant stakeholders into the room. This can be a challenging and tricky process in itself.

Identifying an inclusive list of stakeholders, reaching them and motivating them to come together to explore the problem takes excellent networks, communication skills and lots of time and energy.

Once stakeholders have come together, skilled facilitation is then essential to encourage both inquiry and advocacy. Inquiry is needed so that all stakeholders actively listen to each other, with the facilitator drawing out the different perspectives on the problem through insightful questions and genuine interest.

Advocacy is a skill that allows stakeholders to share, disclose and clearly articulate their personal experiences and perspectives of the dilemma.

Effective facilitation can assist in developing a shared definition of the dilemma that reflects all stakeholder input. Without this shared definition, finding an enduring solution will be impossible. One of the challenges of dilemmas is that they have many different facets. The resulting temptation is for different groups to identify and promote solutions to different aspects of the dilemma, thereby leading to confrontation and argument.

Once a shared definition of the dilemma is achieved, the facilitator needs to extend the exploratory conversations so that each stakeholder has an opportunity to describe what really matters to them about the solution. The decision criteria generated will be invaluable later in the process.

The exploration of the dilemma and the achieving of an agreement on both its scope and the picture of what a "good" solution looks like helps stakeholders understand the perspectives of their fellow collaborators. It assists them in recognising the limitations of their own knowledge and the value that other perspectives can bring. Shared understanding starts to build more positive relationships, trust in each other and trust in the process. These are essential to success in the following steps.

To be able to co-design a process all stakeholders need to agree on a definition of the dilemma and what matters about the solution.

Examples from our personal experience –

Vic Roads inviting the stakeholders into a dilemma

One particular government authority that we have found extremely open to the idea of inviting stakeholders into a perplexing dilemma is the Victorian government's highway agency VicRoads. We were impressed by their willingness to display a degree of vulnerability recently during the redevelopment of the Healesville Freeway.

They freely admitted to the difficult issue that faced them and invited stakeholders in to help understand it. In this instance, the dilemma involved a corridor of land (now no longer needed) that was once purchased by VicRoads for potential freeway development. Not being in the business of land management it was necessary for the agency to realise that asset by selling it. The question was, how? While already under pressure, they were mindful that community members were already upset that they were going to lose what they'd been using as public space.

We suggested to the agency the approach of inviting stakeholders to explore this particular dilemma with them. Their message to their stakeholders was, "We're a government department that doesn't need this land; therefore we need to sell the land and put the proceeds towards other road projects.

From our perspective we need to make the land attractive to potential buyers. This may impact on you in a number of ways. What does this look like from your perspective and can you help us achieve multiple objectives?"

By demonstrating a degree of vulnerability, they didn't have to come up with a solution by themselves and sell it to the community. Community members who were involved in that conversation took up the challenge. They stepped into the space, were willing to share ideas on the question that needed to be asked, agreed on the scope of the dilemma, and set to work on coming up with possible solutions. The process is ongoing.

Seeing the dilemma from both sides in Wingecarribee

The Wingecarribee Shire Council rate rise case study from our Introduction is another example of stakeholders first needing to understand and agree on the dilemma before they could own or advocate for particular solutions.

When Council initially tried to convince their constituents that a rate rise was necessary, the response was negative. But when council subsequently opted to try a collaborative and inclusive study circle approach involving a group of citizens who then arrived at a recommendation to support such a rise, the situation was completely reversed.

This was because those citizens acquired a very strong sense of ownership of first the dilemma and then Council's preferred solution.

B. To help frame the dilemma, stakeholders need to be assured their interests are understood and that the sponsor is genuine

So, what does it take for stakeholders to be both willing and confident to participate in defining the dilemma? In his book What Makes Us Tick, acclaimed Australian social researcher Hugh Mackay says that something that registers highly in the personal importance stakes is the desire to be taken seriously.

We all want our voices to be heard as authentic, legitimate and worthy of attention. We resent being overlooked, dismissed or belittled. Among all the factors that explain why we do the things we do, this is paramount. When we know we're being taken seriously, we can relax in that assurance. When we believe this not to be the case our reactions can range from sadness, resignation and disappointment through to burning fury or resentment.

Another concept that we find useful in this step is that of Appreciative Inquiry, or AI. Appreciative Inquiry differs from a traditional problem-solving approach because of its underlying assumption that people are always evolving, growing and moving forward into the future and that to solve dilemmas or complex and controversial multi-faceted problems it is necessary to harness the capacities, capabilities, resources and strengths of all those with a stake in the solution. Using an appreciative approach means "deliberately asking positive questions to ignite constructive dialogue and inspired action."

An appreciative approach to problem solving is based on a genuine belief in the ability of ordinary people, given both opportunity and encouragement, to understand complex dilemmas and be creative and innovative in finding solutions.

For stakeholders to be willing to work together in a collaborative way, advocate for themselves and inquire of others, share their thoughts and define the dilemma, they must be confident of three things: that their activities will contribute to real change, that they will be provided with the autonomy, independence, space and time to be effective, and that the decision-making body has a serious regard for the collaboration and the outcomes it will deliver.

A lack of confidence at Sydney's Callan Park

Callan Park is both the name of a patch of prime Sydney harbourside real estate and the name of the State-run mental health facility that has inhabited the site for many decades.

Our introduction to Callan Park occurred some ten years ago when we were invited by the State-run land development agency and the then leaders of the Area Health Service to help them work with the community to gain input on a development proposal for the site. The mental health facility, made up of old and out of date buildings that were unsuitable for the administering of modern-day mental health care, was to be closed. The Health Service wanted the land development agency to start a conversation about planning for the very valuable site once the hospital was moved.

We initially undertook some research and explorative work in order to gain a better understanding of the situation. We attended a Callan Park open day where we met some of the local activists who were eager to keep the medical facility exactly where it was. We learned that the building itself, while old and not always well maintained, had an interesting history, both from an architectural and historical standpoint and also as a result of its role as a key mental health care provider.

We were also told that the hospital was home to people who had lived there for a long time and many sympathetic locals felt they shouldn't be moved. It's important to note that no community members had been consulted about the health authority's decision to close Callan Park, and that what we heard that day was an expression of people's response to news stories about the planned closure and a demonstration of what they valued about their locality.

We found that the welfare of patients was only part of the story. The Callan Park site is quite open. It accommodates numerous hospital buildings of varying ages and states of repair and includes a lot of open space that patients enjoy and locals use as parkland to walk their dogs and access the water. Its very openness has provided local open space highly valued by the community. Once it no longer housed a hospital it would be redeveloped to its full potential as a valuable harbourside property.

Upon completing our preliminary fact-finding, we advised the client that the local community was organised and opposed to the closure of the hospital and the transfer of patients to another area of Sydney and were not willing to start any conversation about what might happen to the site once the facility had been moved. We suggested that organising face-to-face meetings designed to provide more information, generate acceptance of the closure and start a conversation on land planning was unlikely to be a successful strategy. The highly educated and angry community members would use such a meeting as an opportunity to vent their anger about a decision that ignored their views. As such, it would constitute a risky and difficult venture.

Despite our advice our client was determined to pursue the traditional community consultation public meeting format. Reluctantly, we agreed to facilitate. As we anticipated, very little was achieved. A large number of very angry people occupied a relatively small space, neither side willing to listen. Deciding that her political future was at risk, the local Labor member took the side of the locals. The mental health facility still operates on the site today.

For us it was a classic example of a situation where the Health Service did not believe in the value of stakeholder input, while stakeholders had no sense of the dilemma faced by the Health Service and were given no role to play in its solution. Not surprisingly, the planned conversation quickly denigrated into an unworkable, emotion-fraught quagmire. The obvious question here is: could the adoption of a different approach and mindset have transformed the situation into an opportunity to arrive at some lasting solutions? We certainly believe so.

A. For stakeholders to be assured, there needs to be a solid commitment to collaborate from the sponsor and a positive mindset

In our many years of working with organisations that needed to engage communities and stakeholders in decision-making, one factor stands out as the necessary pre-condition for successful engagement. Unless the decision-makers within the engaging organisation value the participation of its community and genuinely seek to understand community aspirations, issues and concerns about its proposals that might affect them, the engagement is unlikely to be a positive experience for any of the three participating groups. The organisation resents the time and money spent on an unnecessary activity. The engagement practitioners recognise the disconnect between community input and decision-making. The community is frustrated and dissatisfied when the organisation appears disinterested in their input or ideas.

We believe that the mindset of decision-makers is important. If they recognise the value of stakeholder input and are clear about what input will add value to their decisions, then the experience is likely to be a positive one. If such a mindset doesn't exist, then any discussion of collaboration will be counter-productive.

As we have discussed in Chapter Two, the 'curse of the expert' is a factor that can turn the relationship between organisation and community toxic. When professionals believe that they have all the information and skill necessary to make decisions and that external stakeholders have nothing useful to add, even the best collaborative process will not provide benefits.

For collaboration to be effective and achieve positive outcomes there needs to be a commitment to the process from all levels within the sponsoring organisation - from its political masters, corporate board, CEO and senior executive team, all the way through to its project managers and communications and engagement teams.

For any preparation for collaboration to commence, the organisation must genuinely understand the implications of collaboration and sign a statement of collaborative intent.

Planning for a Sydney Harbour park

About 10 years ago we were commissioned to lead the community engagement to support a planning project for a new public park on Sydney Harbour. The first meeting of the project team included project management, planning and consultation staff from the sponsoring organisation that managed the Sydney Harbour foreshore, plus external landscape architects and horticulturalists. We were all asked to describe our perceived role in the project. When the question was put to us, we inquired what type of input each of the other players wanted from the community, as it was our job to ensure they got it. All the external experts looked puzzled and said that they didn't need anything.

This was the catalyst for a healthy discussion (led by the sponsors) about the role they wanted the community to play in the development of the park. The foreshore authority genuinely wanted to hear from the park's neighbours, the local neighbourhood, as well as the community of harbour users about what they wanted the park to contain. They then wanted to develop some principles and guidelines that the park plan would need to satisfy.

Once the vision and principles were in place, the planners and the park design experts were able to go ahead with a range of possible designs that the community later evaluated against those predetermined principles. Just asking the question at the project team meeting helped everyone understand the authority's mindset about the community's role.

A Masterplan for Sydney Airport

In 2003 it became necessary for Macquarie Bank (who had just bought Sydney Airport) to complete a 20 year master plan as one of the requirements of the sale. This involved identifying key parameters relating to things like the possible addition of runways, the number of plane movements per hour, and flight curfews.

In this case, the decision was taken to spend time up-front engaging with a multitude of relevant stakeholders in order to identify and shape the key questions before the master plan was formulated.

This initial conversation involved a large stakeholder group, including Mayors and CEOs from surrounding Sydney councils, airline and airport representatives, airport users including business commuters and local interest groups including an activist group focused on the impact of noise from plane take-offs and landings on local communities.

This group, together with decision-makers from within Sydney Airport Corporation, took nine months to agree on the question that would be put forward to the Master Plan Citizens' Jury.

From a fairly general question about the future of the airport, the decision the Citizens' Jury was asked to address was: "The founding principle for the Sydney Airport Master Plan is that there will be no change to the basic operating framework of Sydney Airport (that is, there will be no new or altered runways or flight paths, and the legislated curfew and movement cap will remain). Noting that any changes would require stakeholder consultation, is this founding principle appropriate?"

This question gave clarity to both airport managers and the 16 selected jurors about what they could expect. The new owners got the direction they needed in regard to the required 20 year master plan. Characterised by a high level of transparency, preparations for the jury process provided

*an opportunity for decision-makers and stakeholders to be involved in
shaping the question, and engendered confidence in the final report from
the jury process.*

Challenges for Leaders

In a perfect world, getting different groups together to explore dilemmas,
appreciate complexities, share ownership and arrive at solutions that
everyone is happy with would be effortless. In reality, achieving this state
of play is sometimes a very difficult proposition indeed. When managers
don't understand or trust the process, when there is reluctance from those
holding the power to relinquish it, when a command-and-control structure
gets in the way or when those with the power remain determined to make
the decisions, collaboration will have little or no chance of success.

With this in mind, we need to recognise the triggers that may prompt leaders
to hold on tightly to the control levers. It's no secret that hugely complex
issues can have a significant effect on leaders' perspectives. It takes courage
for a leader to be open enough to say, "We can't solve this problem", and
to then invite the group to step into that dilemma, define it and design a
process to solve it together. The reason leaders often return to the traditional
rational problem-solving formula is that they're scared of both the issue
complexity and the level of potential community angst. Not surprisingly, it
seems easier to revert to an approach that's familiar. Therefore, suggesting
the option of co-defining the dilemma with stakeholders can be a big issue.
After all, while it can certainly be hard to say, "I don't know the answer,"
it's even more difficult to say, "I don't even know what the question is". But
determining the problem you're trying to solve from a range of perspectives
is a crucial step towards solving it.

Even when a commitment to collaborate is achieved from the sponsoring
organisation there's still no guarantee of the individuals involved establishing
a fruitful working relationship with stakeholders. For many, it remains a
scary new space, with the prospect of giving up their right to decide on a
way forward being too much to contemplate.

To step into collaboration, an organisation needs what we call an appreciative mindset and an internal culture that rewards collaborative activity and values the contributions of both internal and external stakeholders in finding solutions to problems. In our experience, achieving ownership of both process and outcome requires a mindset that says "this matters".

Getting it right the first time

Leaders and potential ownership sponsors must remember that they only have one chance to make a first impression that will encourage positive participation. Consider the opinion of Dr Vince Covello, Director of the Center for Risk Communication in New York. Dr Covello believes that people decide within 30 seconds who they can trust. If stakeholders or community members in those first seconds sense from verbal and non-verbal cues that decision-makers aren't really open to sharing the dilemma and harnessing their expertise and energy to find a new solution, their willingness to accommodate and participate will rapidly diminish.

This is exactly what we've observed in instances where organisations have reluctantly or begrudgingly agreed to undertake collaborative practice as a result of legislation that virtually forces them to. The resulting mindset and lack of energy ensures that proceedings commence in the worst possible way. Building trust depends on beginning with a mindset that includes a belief that people can bring enormous value and wisdom to solving a problem or dilemma.

Beginning with the end in mind means acknowledging what it takes to make collaboration work and ensuring those things are in place before you start.

The success factors that our experience tells us are important are:

• a mandate to address an issue or group of related issues from a recognised decision-making body which itself has serious regard for the collaboration and will not allow it to be subverted;

• appropriate resourcing with funding coming from the decision-making body; the resources the collaborative process has at its disposal should be utilised for the benefit of the process as a whole;

• stakeholders in the problem may be invited to step in to a collaborative process but will make their own decision whether or not to participate;

• stakeholders who participate in a collaboration must believe they have a real, inescapable and unconstrained responsibility to reach a consensus on a solution to the initial problem;

• participants need to be provided with information on the economic, social, cultural and environmental aspects of the problem to be solved as well as valid, reliable and relevant scientific information in order to allow the participants to come to an integrated understanding about the extent of the problem and the potential solutions;

• participants in a collaboration require autonomy, independence, space and time to do their work;

• parties to a collaborative process must be confident that their work will contribute to real change;

• sufficient time but also time constraints and a realistic timetable;

• collaborative processes must be open and transparent but, at the same time, will inevitably be messy and unpredictable;

• a skilled independent facilitator or chair;

• clarity about participants' individual and shared responsibilities for achieving consensus, approving the report and planning subsequent implementation.

The following chapters will explore each of the steps to Collaborative Governance identified by Twyfords in 2011:

- **Commit to collaboration** by exploring the prevailing mindset, illuminating existing strengths and opportunities, and signing a statement of collaborative intent;

- **Co-define the dilemma** by identifying stakeholders, scoping the dilemma, issue or problem together and describing success from all the diverse stakeholder perspectives;

- **Co-design** process by sharing process options, considering context and resources and co-designing an appropriate and workable governance structure and engagement process;

- **Co-create** solutions by exploring options, evaluating impacts and deliberating decisions;

- **Co-deliver** actions by determining governance structure for implementation, agreeing stakeholder roles, responsibilities and accountabilities;

- Establish a monitoring and evaluation framework.

Alastair Bisley, who ran the New Zealand Land and Water Forum between 2009 and 2011, has suggested that the key steps in forging and completing collaborations are:

- **Defining** the challenge
- **Defining** the collaborators
- **Creating** the space
- **Allowing** the time
- **Recognising** the process will be messy and unpredictable.

We at Twyfords believe the long-term benefits of collaboration come from the trust, positive relationships and new knowledge created.

Trustful relationships, once established and maintained, allow workable governance structures to be established, actions planned and implemented quickly and solutions delivered efficiently.

Key Learnings from Chapter 3

- Beginning with the end in mind is a useful piece of advice, so that each step is built on the outcomes of the previous ones.

- For a solution to be enduring, stakeholders need to have a role in solution implementation.

- To be part of shared solution-making, stakeholders need to participate fully in the process.

- To participate fully, stakeholders need to own (that is, help design) the solution-finding process.

- To co-design the process, stakeholders need to agree on the scope of the dilemma and what matters about its solution.

- To help frame the dilemma, stakeholders need to be assured their interests are understood and that the sponsor is genuine.

- For stakeholders to be assured, there needs to be a solid commitment to collaborate from the sponsor and a positive mindset.

Chapter 4

Step One – Commit to Collaboration

> *"When you change the way you look at things,*
> *the things you look at change."*
>
> Graham Jenkins

> *"The end of all our exploring will be to arrive at where*
> *we began and to know the place for the first time."*
>
> T.S.Eliot

Commit to collaboration by exploring the prevailing mindset, illuminating existing strengths and opportunities, and signing a statement of collaborative intent.

Where should we commence the process of collaborative governance, and what is the catalyst for acknowledging that a different approach is needed?

Our experience suggests that the answers to these two key questions can be found at either end of a continuum. At one extreme, the energy can originate from inside an organisation as a result of collaborative practice experience. Perhaps the organisation has long depended on cross-functional teams working together to achieve better outcomes. Perhaps the organisation has already experienced the value that different perspectives can bring to defining and solving complex and challenging problems.

At the other extreme, an organisation can find itself on "a burning platform"; that is, facing a crisis that threatens its very foundations. As such, traditional methods of problem-solving simply aren't going to work. Perhaps some unexpected advice suggests that there might be a way to work with angry, hostile and confrontational community members or activists so that a solution can be found together. Perhaps leaders are so desperate that they decide, despite reservations, to attempt collaboration because their confrontational alternative is currently trashing relationships and threatening to derail critical projects or processes. Perhaps there is an element of both internal collaborative experience and a crisis that determines a decision to work collaboratively. Whatever the background or motivating drivers, the first step when collaboration is proposed is always the same.

At the outset, it's important to explore what the organisation knows or understands about collaboration and whether there is an openness, willingness and readiness to commit to a collaborative process with stakeholders. Such exploration must involve the senior leadership and those individuals within the organisation who will be responsible for, and accountable for, the final decision. It also needs to involve those people who will take responsibility for the collaborative process and the implementation of the resulting solution.

This exploration needs to take into account a number of issues, such as whether a range of perspectives will help achieve a better understanding of a particular dilemma; whether leaders accept that a solution to a particular complex problem can and should emerge from the capabilities and experiences of others; whether stakeholders co-creating solutions together and making decisions by consensus offers real value in the trust and positive relationships it builds; whether leaders believe in the power of such decision-making processes to improve the quality of decisions and render them more enduring; whether both the relevant individuals and the organisation with the mandate to address a particular issue are committed to collaboration as a way of achieving wise outcomes, and whether mutual trust can be built slowly, step by step through respectful dialogue and shared experiences.

Deciding to step into this collaborative space takes both foresight and courage, not to mention what many would term a radically different mindset. But most of all it takes an understanding of what collaboration means and a genuine intent to collaborate and a willingness to begin.

As part of establishing a commitment to collaborate, it is important to understand who has the ultimate mandate and authority to identify the dilemma and find a solution. Where does the buck stop? Is it with one or more government agencies? Is it with a corporation? Is it with a Governance Group set up specifically for this project? If it is indeed a government agency, does the responsibility sit with the Minister or with the Executive? If it's a corporation, does the responsibility sit with the Board, the Executive, or with someone holding delegated authority? If it's a Governance Group, who is included in the group and who isn't? What is its Terms of Reference and how will its members work together?

It may also be useful to check who or what has ceded the relevant individual or body their authority and whether it can be rescinded before the collaboration has been concluded. When the ultimate decision-maker or decision-makers have been identified, it will then be necessary for their views to be canvassed regarding the proposed collaboration. Do they support collaboration as a way of co-creating an enduring solution? How involved do they want to be in the collaborative process? Will they be part of the collaboration, or will they receive the recommendations of the collaborators? Are they bound to endorse any consensual decision made by the collaborators? If they don't endorse it, do they have to give reasons before setting it aside? Unless the whole organisation, from the Board or the Minister down, is committed to collaboration and the outcomes it produces and understands what that commitment implies, the potential for success is low.

Collaborative practice is challenging. Setting up for success means ensuring that certain things are in place. In our experience success factors include:

• all parties having a serious regard for the collaboration and a determination not to let it be subverted;

• appropriate resourcing that is used for the benefit of the process as a whole;

• a shared belief that stakeholders who participate have a real, inescapable and unconstrained responsibility to reach consensus on a solution to the initial dilemma;

- the organisation providing sufficient autonomy, independence, space and time for the collaboration; and

- a shared confidence that the outcomes of the collaboration will contribute to real change.

It's essential that both the willingness and readiness of the organisation to step into a genuinely collaborative process be explored. Tools are available to support this exploration and give leaders and managers either the confidence in their capability to succeed or the realisation that collaboration is not the right approach because the organisational mindset and culture is not ready.

In our experience the ability to make this conceptual leap depends on leaders having what we term an 'appreciative mindset'. With this mindset leaders acknowledge that the broader perspective of stakeholders and community (rather than just a small, elitist group of experts), holds the potential to co-create the desired answers. When leaders acknowledge this, the collaborative process appears safer to stakeholders and becomes a welcoming space where everyone feels personally respected as a contributor.

Exploring existing mindsets for the appreciative spark and then fanning it into a flame within the organisation and among stakeholders is necessary for collaborative success. Telling stories of positive experiences of successful teamwork or partnerships can generate energy and enthusiasm for a different approach and create a base on which collaborative practice can be built.

Successful solution generation is about tapping into the greater knowledge and discretionary energy that all people have to both appreciate and solve a dilemma. Examples of this discretionary energy are everywhere. For instance, a colleague once related a story that took place during his career in industry. In order to solve a particular problem on the production line, one operator actually designed a solution in his home workshop. He did this because none of the engineers at work believed that this problem could be solved without serious technical expertise, so didn't ask operators for their ideas. Yet one operator solved the problem on his own, in his own time, with his own equipment using the knowledge and skill gained in his daily operational work. It was a classic example of the positive use, or release, of discretionary energy.

Another recent example of effective discretionary energy release involves a group of ordinary people who are very afraid of the potential environmental disaster that might result from exploration and extraction of coal seam gas. They have spent their energy creating a parody website mirroring the Australian Petroleum Production and Extraction Association (APPEA) site at wewantcsg.com.au.

Their URL www.wewantcsg.org, as well as their design including text, photographs and videos, have been carefully selected to make their points. Their campaign required energy, enthusiasm, skills and resources, all of which the individuals involved had the discretion to either commit or withhold. This kind of individual energy exists in all communities. Leaders don't need to create it. They just have to find a way to tap into it.

The key to tackling the kind of complex issues this book is about is appreciating that people often possess unexpected perspectives or have innovative ideas to solve a problem they care about. People can be creative, energetic and generous. People will take good solutions forward and make them stick if they believe in them and own them. The trick for leaders is to trigger the release point for all that discretionary energy, to tap into that through an appreciative mindset.

Of course, the release of this energy can be off-putting for some. When someone unexpected comes up with an innovative solution, some leaders may feel that they're losing control. If we think about the case of the operator who solved a problem that the experts had struggled to overcome, it's easy to see that the engineers may have felt shown up. Likewise, APPEA leaders are unlikely to give credit to their opposition for their parody website. It takes effort and generosity of spirit to overcome pride and hubris and acknowledge creativity or insight from an unlikely or unexpected source.

When decision-makers learn how to recognise and take advantage of discretionary energy they can unleash unexpected actions. However, complex problems need systemic solutions as well as creative energy.

Leaders with an appreciative mindset will understand the value of focusing the whole system on the problem, thus allowing a solution to emerge from any source.

It's all in the numbers

Do more people and perspectives really mean wiser or better quality decisions? The wisdom of crowds has been recognised by thinkers and researchers throughout the ages. One example of this recognition is referred to in one of our favourite books, actually called *"The Wisdom of Crowds – Why the many are smarter than the few and how collective wisdom shapes business, economies, societies and nations"*, by James Surowiecki.

Surowiecki tells the story of British scientist Francis Galton who, one day in 1906, left his home in Plymouth to attend the annual West of England Fat Stock and Poultry Exhibition, a regional fair where local farmers and townspeople gathered to appraise the quality of each other's cattle, sheep, poultry, horses and pigs. Wandering through the various displays, he came upon a competition that involved guessing the weight of an ox.

Galton saw this as an opportunity to undertake some research to confirm his view that democracy was a dangerous idea and demonstrate that specialists with authority and good educations should be trusted to make key decisions. Galton believed that the livestock experts attending the Exhibition would be able to estimate the animal's weight with the greatest accuracy. However, also taking part in the competition were 800 locals or non-experts for whom the notion of guessing an ox's weight was a novelty. The ox, when slaughtered and dressed, weighed 1195 pounds, and Galton was right. Those who had estimated a weight closest to the actual figure were indeed those who traded in livestock. However Galton then added up the 800 other guesses and divided the sum by number of entries, and incredibly, arrived at a figure that was almost exactly the ox's weight. The surprising result showed him that while the correct answer did not lie with any one individual, it lay collectively with the crowd. Together, they knew the answer. Together, they were more accurate than the most expert among the experts. Recognising the wisdom of crowds, provided that certain criteria are met, lies at the heart of an appreciative mindset.

It's not so easy

At a recent conference we attended, the word 'collaboration' was used frequently. The speakers were describing a necessary strategy to achieve solutions that work, but they gave no hint of the 'how' of collaboration. As we described in the previous chapter our experience is that leaders who are used to being in control do not find the practice of collaboration easy. Faced with a complex problem such leaders often revert to approaches that are familiar because they are nervous, anxious or even scared of the consequences of getting the answer wrong, or of trusting other people to find a solution that evades the 'experts'.

Overriding familiar patterns of behaviour requires self-control and reasoning. When a leader's experience is that a particular way of solving problems has been useful in the past, they are likely to think it will be useful in the future. They believe arguments that support what they already believe even when they are unsound. They do not always take the trouble or have sufficient motivation to be sceptical about their intuitions of familiarity.

As Daniel Kahneman attests in his book "Thinking Fast and Slow", employing an effort of will is tiring. As a result, a leader may be less willing to repeat the effort when the next challenge comes along. This behavioural phenomenon is known as "ego depletion". A leader whose ego is depleted, perhaps after a long day of meetings, is less likely to utilise mental energy (or System Two thinking) to solve the next problem and may well revert to an approach that's familiar even though it may not provide the best outcomes.

In particular, leaders are often blind to the need to share perspectives on the problem itself. But exploring an issue from a range of perspectives is a crucial step towards defining the problem. Only then can it be fully understood and a solution determined.

Bertrand Russell, one of the 20th century's greatest thinkers, is quoted as saying "The greatest challenge to any thinker is stating the problem in a way that will allow a solution." Understanding how others perceive the problem is vital in being able to define it.

We must also recognise that even after leaders are convinced and a commitment to collaborate is achieved, there's still no guarantee they will establish a fruitful working relationship with stakeholders. Experiencing a loss of the control they are used to can be scary, with the prospect of giving up their right to decide on a way forward being too much for a traditional leader to contemplate.

But a truly collaborative process requires an appreciative mindset, where leaders welcome a diverse range of perspectives and contributions and understand the value of sharing the dilemma and the way through it. Leveling the power playing field and developing positive relationships with stakeholders that build trust over time are essential precursors to genuine collaboration.

The Occasional Roadblock
As we have discussed in Chapter Two, the 'curse of the expert' is a factor that can turn the relationship between organisation and community toxic. When professionals believe that they have all the information and skill necessary to make decisions and external stakeholders have nothing useful to add, even the best collaborative process will not provide benefits.

However, claims by anyone that they are the expert and have all the necessary knowledge and skill to solve a problem is likely to be taken by colleagues more as a sign of arrogance and hubris than genuine genius. Luckily, with its inherent promise of shared ideas and new learning, the concept of collective wisdom is a comforting idea for many leaders.

However, standing in the way of a possible collaboration with stakeholders may be previous negative experiences of verbal attacks or organisational battering. Such unpleasant and uncomfortable experiences can trigger resistance to further attempts at connecting, building relationships, or working collaboratively with those people who may have given them a hard time in the past.

We came across one such example several years ago –

A local council over a period of 20 years had developed a difficult relationship with a small but active group of community members whose "Council bashing" activities had been exhaustively reported in the media. Councillors and Council staff had retreated behind barriers and were no longer even attempting to communicate across them. With negative sentiment pervading all levels of the council hierarchy, communication had broken down entirely. It was a classic portrait of a battered organisation.

However, eventually the long-serving General Manager moved on and his role was temporarily filled by an internal staff member. Soon we were having conversations with senior managers who were saying things like, "There's a new breeze blowing through the place." Before long we were planning a set of community workshops. We recommended obtaining input to the process through a series of telephone or face-to-face interviews with constituents that included some of the Council's previous critics. The acting general manager volunteered to make some of the calls. Amazingly, he subsequently reported that he had grown up in the same Melbourne suburb as one of the most belligerent members of the activist group. Moreover, both supported the same football team and their fathers actually knew each other. All of a sudden there was a connection, highlighting for him and his colleagues that those on the outside were just people after all.

The different approach to community relations that resulted from the change of leadership and organisational mindset meant a change within the community as well. All of a sudden people were easier to work with. They attended the workshops that were designed after the research was completed and contributed positively, constructively, and optimistically to first identifying and then addressing the dilemma that faced the area. The only thing that changed was the mindset of all involved. It began with the Council leader and almost instantly permeated the entire organisational culture. Almost as quickly, constructive conversation with their community (and the chance to really get things done) was possible.

Getting What You Expect

The 'Pygmalion Effect' refers to a body of research carried out in the 1950's that graphically illustrates the way in which people can live up to whatever expectations we place on them. The setting for the experiment was a classroom where the children on one side of the room were labeled as being exceptionally bright, creative, and clever, and therefore in need of much encouragement and intellectual stimulation. Their teacher was told that regardless of indications to the contrary, they were to be pushed as far as possible. The children on the other side of the room, meantime, were presented as being less academically bright, with the teacher therefore instructed to keep things simple and not to expect too much from them.

Within a short period of time the supposedly bright group was completely outperforming the other even though both groups constituted children of similar ability levels. They had been grouped randomly without reference to any recognised ability. The key variable in play was the level of expectation placed on their performance. Those who were expected to perform well did so. Those who were expected to be average were just that.

The same principle can be applied to working with stakeholders and communities. Consultation processes are often designed and constructed according to the expectation that people will behave at their very worst. If bad behaviour is expected, there is a tendency to design processes to manage those behaviours. We box people in and tell them they must do this or they can't do that. The process feels manipulative and stakeholders react badly. It inevitably becomes a self-fulfilling prophecy. The organisation sees the stakeholders' bad behaviour and feels justified in its negative views. The stakeholders feel manipulated and feel justified in their lack of trust and determination to stop whatever they fear.

However, if decision-makers expect the best of people, believe in their capabilities, their creativity, their ability to look at things from a range of perspectives, their willingness to engage in a civic-minded way or look at the whole picture, the process design and the actions and attitudes of both the leaders and the engagement practitioners will reflect that belief. Stakeholders will pick up those messages very quickly. Relationships will become more positive, trust will develop, slowly at first, and opportunities will open up for far more constructive and collaborative processes.

The Council example above is a case in point. For years, they treated the community just as some members of the community treated Council – as enemies. One week, the General Manager and staff perceived their constituent community as being inhabited by a group of aggressive, angry, misguided people who had no understanding of the work Council did and the constraints they faced in meeting everyone's expectations. With a new leader and a different mindset, community members were treated as people who could co-create a vision for their city, so they did.

On an international scale, the person who has demonstrated himself to be arguably the greatest appreciative mindset practitioner is Nelson Mandela.

Mandela served as President of South Africa from 1994 to 1999 and was the first South African president to be elected in a fully representative democratic election.

He inherited a country occupied by two warring factions (the blacks who had been oppressed by white rule for 100 years, and the whites who were now petrified by the idea that the blacks would hold the power). It was a complex situation that could easily have erupted in violence and bloodshed.

However, the establishment of the South African Truth and Reconciliation Commission brought people from both sides to face one another and talk about what it had been like under the previous system.

This was not done with a view of punishing the perpetrators of violence, but to facilitate a shared understanding of what it would have been like to be on the other side. The process also acknowledged that everyone had a vital role to play. It was about ensuring that stories were told in a room occupied by the very people who were either responsible for, or suffered from, the previous regime.

When it came to involving himself in the process, Mandela must have believed that people were capable of rising to the occasion. He'd already spent 27 years in jail getting to know his jailers and had said that gaining an understanding of the enemy was necessary. If all you could do was to talk to your jailers, then you did so.

Leaders such as Mandela have great compassion. Such individuals realise that people are the way they are because of their life journeys and the experiences that have shaped their world views. Such leaders are prepared to accept this reality and then search for ways of achieving something better than the individual parts.

When leaders make a visible and tangible commitment to collaborate, stakeholders are likely to make a similar commitment. And if the decision-makers thoughtfully and respectfully listen to what their stakeholders have to tell them, stakeholders can step into a different space that allows everyone to address and move on past the issues that have historically blocked progress.

Importantly, the appreciative mindset is not just necessary at the beginning of a process. Positive relationships and trust can only be built slowly step by step through respect and shared experiences throughout the collaboration. These trustful relationships are a significant benefit for both parties. Trust within and between groups leads to the fast tracking of future collaborative processes. Energy and time aren't needed to build relationships and people already work together in a positive way.

Choosing Your Perspective

Social researcher Hugh Mackay's second law of human communication states that people will interpret things in the way that makes them feel safe and secure. When we believe something it's not difficult to find enough evidence to confirm this point of view. If you believe that people are inherently selfish and ignorant, you'll look for evidence to support that opinion, and what you find will almost certainly both reflect and reinforce your belief.

Appreciative Inquiry tells us that the things we focus on grow. Change the focus and you change what grows. Choose to focus on people's capabilities, skills, aspirations and values and how they can benefit a situation and you will find a way forward.

One of the techniques that we've found useful for establishing this mindset has been suggested by David Cooperrider in his work on Appreciative Inquiry. The technique involves asking improbable pairs of people to interview each other about what their best experiences have been in regard to interacting with a person, group, or organisation. Using this approach, we often find that while people have negative baggage or a history of unpleasant experiences, they will also have recollections of instances that can be classed as distinctly positive. With those experiences identified, the next logical step is to pinpoint just what it was that made it work. In this sense, we are not imposing an expert model for someone else to adopt. We're saying, "Let's identify your strengths, your experiences and what you know works and see how we might apply it in this particular situation." This approach also reduces the trepidation associated with heading into the unfamiliar. All it requires is the decision to focus on the positive.

We applied this model during our work with the New Zealand Transit Authority, where one of the participants told a positive story about a journey that was, on the surface, anything but pleasant. It all took place when this person had been driving from Auckland to Wellington during a period of particularly treacherous wet weather. Washed-out roads necessitated a series of detours, one of which resulted in a collision with a traffic sign that was lying on the road, damaging his car.

To make matters even worse, he ended up being 12 hours late to his intended destination. It certainly qualified as the trip from hell. However, an element of positivity arose when he subsequently approached the relevant local council over the incident. They acknowledged that a sign lying in the middle of the road was their responsibility, and duly paid compensation. This unexpected response left him feeling positive.

Clearly, it would have been very easy for the individual in question to focus on the highly negative aspect of his experience. However, a positive appreciative mindset helped him and the others in the group move into a solution-orientated mode because they were appreciated not only for their stories, but also for the fact they were able to identify the bit that worked. A commitment to tap into people's experiences indicates a belief that those experiences can lead us to more useful outcomes.

We had a similar experience at a recent community forum in a northern Sydney suburb, which was attended by 30 mostly retired and elderly people. One of the residents showed up early with a thick file containing documents dating back to 2006 relating to trees, plans, and policies. His opening salvo was something along the lines of: "What's this meeting about? Is it about this project (pulling out a document)? Because Council has done nothing about that. Or is it about this one? Or this one?"

On being informed that the meeting was about how Council might better engage with its communities he became curious. And although he had attended the meeting to bash Council with a thick file detailing how Council had failed him over the years, by the end of the night he was making valuable contributions. Again, nobody dwelt on his negative experiences. Rather, he was asked to share a story about a good experience that he'd had with Council and listen to other similar stories. His input was valued, he learned something new and the discussions remained positive.

Convincing protagonists that their contribution was valued was also a factor when working in a small NSW country town. In this instance, the local water authority proposed to disconnect the piped water supply and provide households with water tanks instead. This plan was developed in response to problems with the maintenance of a water pipe and a reservoir. Many of the town's residents were angry and upset. At the first community meeting our clients presented their proposal for discussion. A man from the community was in the process of setting up a microphone stand and recording equipment. It was clear he wasn't happy. He said, "I'm going to record everything you say. I don't trust any of you and I want a record of what you say".

Our clients, already nervous about the likely response to their proposal, turned around and walked out, their worst fears seemingly confirmed. Once outside the meeting hall we asked them, 'Why are you worried about being recorded? Are you planning on telling any lies?' Their response was that they didn't like this community member's attitude. Furthermore, what if he went away and edited the tape so severely that he effectively altered their message? Clearly, this was a textbook example of expecting the absolute worst in people.

In response, we suggested going back in and asking the gentleman in question to go and make a copy of his tape immediately after proceedings concluded, and to then bring that copy straight back, thereby reassuring the officials that he would have no opportunity to edit it. They agreed. We then suggested that we go into the meeting and publicly thank him for offering his contribution to the process. Indeed, an accurate record of everything said in the meeting would be an invaluable tool for later reference. This request clearly surprised the man and his community colleagues and helped establish a positive working environment where people felt that their contribution was valued.

This simple strategy diffused things nicely. We and our client built some positive relationships and in the following meetings both the clients and the community were more relaxed and less defensive.

The way we think influences the way we act

Working in this field we sometimes hear terminology from our clients that worries us. Indeed, hearing stakeholders referred to by such descriptions as "squeaky wheels", "the usual suspects", "NIMBY" (Not In My Back Yard), or "CAVE" people (Citizens Against Virtually Everything), certainly doesn't provide us with confidence that mutual respect exists between our client organisation and their constituents. Other phrases we hear in typical engagement situations include people "pursuing their own interests", people with "vested interests" and people who are "just plain ignorant". However, using negative labels constitutes a significant barrier to trustful relationships and useful dialogue.

The practice of 'demonising' others can provide an excuse for under-achievement. While it can make some people feel good in the short-term, such benefits come at a cost because name-calling and negative labeling creates a significant barrier to achieving good outcomes. Hearing staff within an organisation claim that they "can't get a result because the community will never understand or accept the inevitable" makes us wonder whether they can't get a result because of the relationship dynamic they have set up as a result of such labeling.

Part of exploring the appreciative mindset entails testing the assumptions that we hold about other people. One technique we use is to ask a client, 'Who wouldn't you want in the meeting?' In essence, we ask them to identify all the people they might categorise as the enemy and then ascertain the reasons for that perception. We often find that judgements have been made on very little information or even just a single conversation.

Part of helping people step towards an appreciative mindset and explore their negative perceptions involves encouraging them to visualise what positive stakeholder relationships might look like. We might suggest clients ask themselves questions like: *"How good would it feel if people trusted us to do the right thing, worked with us rather than against us and gave us a social license to operate? What difference would that make to our business?"*

Having established the potential value of stakeholders to our business, we are more likely to change the way we think about them and act towards them. It gives us alternative pathways. If we believe stakeholders have inherent wisdom, we will go looking for it and very likely find evidence of it. This will encourage us to want to tap into it. This may take us along quite different pathways and provide us with many different ways of working with stakeholders.

The rationale for the call to commit
Even after achieving an agreement in principle to collaborate, it's still not always easy to take a leadership team or an organisation on the appreciative mindset journey. However, a willingness to dip their toe in the water and say, 'we have nothing to lose here' is often the breakthrough necessary to make a start. To achieve a genuinely appreciative mindset leaders and decision-makers need to experience it and its benefits for themselves. That is, they need an opportunity to try something, test it and find that it has the potential to allow the appreciative spark to fully ignite.

Ultimately, as with most things in life, taking a risk or doing something that's unfamiliar, scary, or uncomfortable requires a deliberate act. The choice to give something a go with an open mind has to be made. To encourage this simple but not always easy step underlines the art of the facilitator. A facilitator of collaborative processes brings with them a belief in and commitment to both the process and the collaborators. Every time a facilitator walks into an engagement forum he or she thinks and acts as though everyone present can and will contribute to the issue at hand while behaving exceptionally well. This approach is generally catching, and the collaborators rise to the occasion and exceed expectations almost every time.

By the end of Step One, it's necessary to have achieved an appreciative mindset toward stakeholders and a solid commitment to collaborate from the sponsoring organisation, its policy makers, strategists, planners and project managers before progressing to Step Two. Unless the decision-makers within the sponsoring organisation value a partnership with their stakeholders and are prepared to share both the power and the decisions, any attempts at a successful collaboration will fail. For collaboration to be effective and achieve positive outcomes a commitment is required within the sponsoring organisation, from its political masters or its corporate board, from its CEO and senior executive team, from its project managers and from its communications and engagement teams.

This is because it's vital that stakeholders believe that their participation is important, that they are partners in the process, and that the sponsor is genuine. They won't believe this just because they are told it's the case. They will believe it only when the behaviour of everyone they meet from within that organisation models authentic collaborative behaviour.

We all want our voices to be heard as authentic, legitimate and worthy of attention. We resent being overlooked, dismissed or belittled. Among all the factors that explain why people do the things they do, this is paramount.

When stakeholders know they are being taken seriously, they can step into a collaborative process with energy and enthusiasm because they can see a way that their interests and ideas can be part of the solution. When stakeholders are invited to collaborate and then find the collaboration is not genuine their reactions can range from sadness, resignation and disappointment through to burning fury or resentment.

The commitment to collaborate can be made tangible through documentation. We suggest that a Statement of Collaborative Intent be drawn up and signed by the ultimate decision maker. This may be a relevant government minister, board chairperson or chief executive. Signing a commitment to collaborate also helps to cement the team's approach to collaboration and include those who will manage the collaborative project and provide its technical and communicative support. This Statement of Collaborative Intent is a document that will focus the minds of all who work on the project, establish a framework for the collaboration process and provide confidence to the stakeholders when they are invited to step into the process during Step Two.

Key Learnings from Chapter 4

• People appreciate being taken seriously

• If you believe stakeholders have inherent wisdom, you look for it, and are likely to find it

• An appreciative mindset acknowledges that the broader perspective of stakeholders and community holds the potential to co-create enduring solutions

• A belief that everyone can and will contribute to such solutions encourages behaviours that deliver authentic collaboration

Chapter 5

Step Two – Co-defining the Dilemma

> *"At its heart, good governance is about strong relationships and shared understandings..."*
>
> Meredith Edwards

Co-define the dilemma by identifying stakeholders, scoping the issue or problem together and describing success from all the diverse stakeholder perspectives.

Searching for solutions is exciting. It's something that many people love to do. Sometimes people love the challenge of finding solutions so much they spend time engaged in the practice even before they have an actual problem to solve. However, this book is about collaborating to solve particular kinds of problems – the ones that are complex and potentially controversial. We refer to these as dilemmas.

As we discussed in Chapter One, dilemmas have particular characteristics that render them much more of a challenge to solve. Therefore, we believe that a particular kind of process is required.

In our previous chapter we put forward the case for leaders adopting an appreciative mindset, one that values the participation of stakeholders in finding a solution to a dilemma to ensure that the solution can be implemented and become an enduring answer to the complex problem.

In this chapter we put forward the case for leaders or ultimate decision-makers sharing what they believe to be the nature of the dilemma with those who are considered to have a stake in it, its resolution, and an agreed starting place for the collaborative process.

The second step in Collaborative Governance includes three actions:

First, identify the stakeholders who have something of value to contribute to the solution and invite them in to the dilemma as it has been defined by the organisation or agency with a mandate to solve it.

Second, focus on defining the dilemma together. If it's a complex dilemma then it's likely the way it has been defined in Step One will not coincide with other stakeholders' point of view. One person's perspective is likely to be different from another's and it is important to bring all the perspectives together and then agree on a definition.

Third, once the definition of the dilemma is agreed upon, spend time finding out what matters about the solution to each of the stakeholders.

Let's take these actions one by one.

Stakeholder identification and invitation:
Identifying the stakeholders who have something of value to contribute and inviting them in to the collaboration sounds simple enough. However, our experience as well as anecdotal evidence from others who have embarked on significant collaborative processes indicates that it needs careful thought and good process, both to identify who the "right" stakeholders are and then to get them in the room together.

Alastair Bisley, Chair of New Zealand's Land and Water Forum, writes in a "Note on Collaboration" (March 2011) that his process was open to all interested groups to send their own representatives, and that Land and Water Forum members largely nominated themselves.

However, in order to nominate or decide to participate, interested groups must first be informed that someone has identified a dilemma, acknowledged them as a stakeholder and is co-ordinating a collaborative process to find a solution before they can put up their hands to participate. This can be another challenge.

In our experience it is often necessary to spend face-to-face time with stakeholder organisations explaining the background and the evidence for a problem existing and inviting them into the collaboration.

In a recent set of recommendations to a client we suggested that a team of people is required to undertake this work. Our suggestion included the need for one person in the team to represent the sponsoring organisation. That person should be able to give reasons for their commitment to a collaborative process. Another person needs to bring knowledge and expertise around the content of the collaboration. In the case of, say, a medical issue, then a local leader in the medical field needs to be able to give credibility to the collaboration as an appropriate way of finding solutions to the dilemma. In the advent of a land use dilemma, a city planner might be the person who provides the information about the problem, the planning processes and how the collaborative process might apply. Finally, the third person needs to bring knowledge of the collaborative process to give confidence to the stakeholders that the process offers them a genuine opportunity to participate and make a difference to the outcome.

This three-member team requires time, resources and a knowledge of the community of interest to be able to meet with stakeholders and share with them the opportunities provided by the collaboration, either encouraging them to nominate (as in the Land and Water Forum example) or inviting them to some kind of stakeholder event at which information about the collaboration can be provided and invitations extended to step into the process.

Another more iterative method of identifying and inviting stakeholders into the dilemma is one suggested by Appreciative Inquiry practitioners on leading large group change. The authors suggest that the process used for planning and facilitating change must be congruent with the desired outcomes, so introducing potential stakeholders into a dilemma needs to be highly participatory and experiential while also reflecting and modeling the behaviour anticipated in the collaborative process. Thus the process might start wherever the energy for collaboration is greatest. Possibly an individual, possibly a small group within the sponsoring organization, will themselves make contact with two or three key stakeholders they know well and believe will be interested in the dilemma as initially defined. This group might grow though conference calls or face-to-face meetings, with each occasion facilitating more shared perspectives on the dilemma. This might then generate a larger group who will learn more about the process of collaborative governance and the way it might pave the way to an enduring solution.

Eventually, a well-informed group of people who have an interest in exploring and solving the dilemma using a collaborative process come together to share the work involved. This would include connecting with the key stakeholders, providing information about the dilemma and the collaboration, and inviting them in.

There is no one right way of identifying and inviting stakeholders to collaborate. Any process needs to reflect the philosophy of the collaboration and model the kind of collaborative behaviour expected from stakeholders.

Appreciative Stakeholder Analysis

One useful tool to help identify stakeholders is what we call an appreciative stakeholder analysis. Once a list of potential stakeholders has been drawn up (this might include government agencies at any of the relevant levels, commercial enterprises from the private and SME sectors, non-government organisations, professional and community organisations as well as individuals), we suggest an analysis of each stakeholder group or individual from the perspective of their potential to add value to the collaboration. The question for the analysis would be, 'If this stakeholder group chose to collaborate fully and with energy throughout the process, what could they add to the process?' The closer the relationship between the sponsoring organisation and the stakeholder groups, the more accurate this analysis is likely to be.

The outcome provides useful insights regarding stakeholder prioritisation - how to reach them, how to create the information they need in order for them to understand the dilemma, and how to invite them into whatever activity will be used to bring them together.

An appreciative analysis of known stakeholders often helps to flush out ideas, not only around an appreciation of how the stakeholder can contribute usefully and add value to the process, but also about stakeholders who might have been missed.

Understanding and appreciating the value that known stakeholders can provide creates a framework that enables gaps to be identified. For example, we have worked on several projects where local councils or government agencies have had to make sensitive decisions about whether or not to approve development applications for schools in certain areas.

In one case this involved a school for children of Muslim families. In another case it entailed a school for teenagers with behavioural problems. The prevailing sensitivity typically stemmed from a perception that the schools and their activities would negatively impact the local community in some way. This concern was often expressed in general rather than specific terms. Working through an appreciative analysis of known stakeholders has allowed a positive exploration of the value that particular stakeholders can add to the process, including known and perhaps feared and demonised activist groups who have been vociferous in their promotion of negative outcomes.

Appreciative questions in such situations have included:

- What principles or values does this group/individual espouse?

- Who are the active and less active members of this group?

- What stake does this group/individual think it has in the dilemma and its resolution?

- What information and perspective does this group/individual have now that would add value to our understanding of the dilemma? (Local knowledge, local history, local values, technical knowledge).

- What other resources might they bring to this process and to the final solution?

- If this group/individual stepped into this dilemma and collaborated fully in all stages, what value could their contribution add?

- How can this group be supported and acknowledged within the collaboration to help them contribute fully?

- What is the status of the relationship between the sponsor and this group/individual? What needs to change in order to achieve the best outcome?

- Who does this group/individual relate to? With whom do they have the strongest links?

Researching the answers to these questions and considering stakeholders from a more appreciative perspective helps give the sponsoring organisation more confidence about the value of bringing diverse perspectives into the process. Appreciating what each stakeholder can bring to a solution and what can be achieved together provides confidence in the process itself, and helps to identify what other perspectives need to be included.

It is extremely important to make sure that the deal-breakers as well as the dealmakers are identified and encouraged to be part of the collaboration.

Anyone who has the power to veto the outcome of the collaboration needs to be involved. All this considered, it is equally important to understand who should not be part of the collaboration. Alastair Bisley has suggested that sometimes it may be necessary to provide a different role for bureaucrats, such as that of "active observer" with no role in any consensus, if there is a risk that their particular position will influence other stakeholders.

Once all the stakeholders who have agreed to be part of the collaborative process have been identified, it is useful for all collaborators, the sponsoring organisation, collaborating stakeholders as well as those who will be facilitating and supporting the collaborative process, to take part in an introductory session which outlines the collaborative governance model and allows an exploration of the roles and responsibilities of each participant. At this time a statement of the dilemma from the sponsoring organisation's perspective can be provided as a starting point for thinking about the dilemma from all stakeholder perspectives.

There are many activities and techniques documented in training and change management literature that have been devised to encourage stakeholders to 'walk in another's shoes for a day' with a view to better understanding perspectives on the dilemma. These activities are important at the start of the process as they enable stakeholders to humanise each other and better understand the range of positions, interests, values and drivers in play.

Activities that help each group illuminate may involve identifying occasions when they've had a successful experience of collaborating with others to get good outcomes; when they have listened rather than talked and the difference it made; when hearing a story from someone they feared or disliked changed that person's image and made them approachable; when acknowledging that there are different perspectives on an issue is a big step forward for a stakeholder with a very narrow focus. All these constitute 'moments of truth' for participants that will allow them to take an appreciative and collaborative approach to solving a complex dilemma.

All of these activities serve to develop relationships and a better understanding among the stakeholders prior to exploring how each of them perceives the dilemma. This approach seems to have a calming effect on those involved. An increased awareness of other stakeholders and their perspectives followed by the opportunity to share their understanding of the dilemma decreases the likelihood of individual participants later jockeying for positions to ensure the success of their ideas. In essence, it sets the scene for a constructive collaborative environment.

The important thing is encouraging stakeholders to commit to collaborate in the same way as we have sought commitment from leaders and decision-makers within the sponsoring organisation in Step One. This commitment comes from creating an environment in which everyone can work together to clarify the dilemma and define it in a way that includes all perspectives.

If people know they will have a chance to listen to others and also be heard, and that the dilemma does indeed reflect the issues and concerns that everybody has, then they are more likely to commit to working together using their collective skills and energy to co-create a solution.

Going Slow to Go Fast

One of the biggest traps decision-makers can fall into is the urge to rush to solutions without first taking the time to appreciate the scope or the complexities of the dilemma. We see this occurring frequently; so frequently, in fact, that we have a name for it - "campaign rush". This describes a state of mind where a sense of urgency and inspiration can actually work against finding a solution that sticks.

In this chapter we want to talk about the importance of stepping back from that rush and taking the time to explore what the dilemma looks like, first from a single perspective, and then from multiple perspectives. A couple of examples from our own experience can help make this point.

When working in a country town in Victoria we were asked to help a Council facing an insurance problem. Roots from the big shady trees that had lined the wide main street since the town was established were pushing up the pavements. The resulting cracks were causing residents to trip and fall. People in wheelchairs or parents with prams were complaining about the difficulties of maneuvering over the cracked and broken surface.

Council's initial solution was to remove the trees, take out the tree roots and resurface the pavements. It proceeded to put this proposal to its community stating the problem in terms of a solution: "We need to remove the trees from the main street." Not surprisingly, despite trying hard to justify their proposal with technical data, they found themselves with an outraged community who loved the trees and did not want their leafy shade removed. After angry and emotional public meetings, Council stepped back and reconsidered the situation. They sought the advice of an arborist who examined the trees and agreed that some of them were diseased and should be removed. They spent time listening to the different community voices and they talked to their own road engineers and town planners. Eventually they reframed the dilemma as: "How can we all enjoy the main street safely?" This lead to some creative options being explored and in the end, while some trees were removed and many were trimmed, most of them remain today, with roads and pavements reconstructed to make the main street a safe place for cars, cyclists and pedestrians.

Another experience was our earlier case study (referred to in Chapter Four) - another excellent example that illustrates the value of understanding the dilemma as opposed to simply jumping straight to a solution.

You may recall that this instance involved a local water authority that informed their eommunity that their existing dam-sourced water supply would have to be terminated due to a report that the 42 kilometres of pipeline infrastructure from the dam to the town was damaged and leaking valuable water. With the town boasting a permanent population of only 40 people, spending the estimated four million dollars required to replace the pipeline simply wasn't a financially viable proposition. However, it was necessary to both stop the water loss and provide safe water to residents.

Consequently, there was a rush to come up with a solution. In this case, that solution took the form of individual home water storage tanks. Not surprisingly, there was a lot of concern and reaction from many community members because they didn't want to install new water tanks. Furthermore, they weren't sure that the pipeline was so badly damaged that it needed to be closed down.

The water authority had made no attempt to explore the problem from anything other than a technical water engineering perspective.

Somewhat reluctantly, the authority decided that it would work with community members as well as its water experts and engineers to undertake an investigation into the structural integrity of the pipeline. As part of the investigation, a group of people drove and walked most of its 42 kilometre length. Ultimately, they found that the pipeline wasn't in such bad condition after all and required only minimal repairs. But more importantly, they found that some people were engaged in illegally tapping into the pipeline for irrigation purposes. It was this practice, and not any structural shortcomings, that was the cause of the massive water loss between the dam and the town reservoir.

The authorities had been trying to solve the wrong problem. Once the actual problem was identified, working together to create a solution was easy. Today, the pipeline continues to supply water, while a degree of community vigilance has put an end to the illegal water tapping practices. Significantly, several years of angst and uncertainty could have been avoided if the water authority had taken the first step to identify its stakeholders and share the dilemma with them.

What a good Dilemma Question looks like

In a January 2012 radio interview, John Paul Lederach, Professor of International Peacebuilding at the Joan B. Kroc Institute for International Peace Studies at the University of Notre Dame, talked about the need to reframe a conflict as a question that holds all the elements of the conflict in tension. He contended that enduring change was linked to the quality of the relationships between unlikely people.

In describing a scene where a group of stakeholders assembled to resolve a conflict about the use of a local resource, he suggested that the question for all parties, rather than being, "Who has the right to use wood and forest resources among the groups here?" could instead be "How can we, together, conserve the forest and at the same time ensure the life-hood and livelihood of the people here?" Such a question had the power to bring together those whose livelihoods were being encroached upon with those who were using forest resources to survive. The resulting conversation was more likely to bring about co-operation and change than any confrontation about rights of use.

In our view a dilemma is often usefully framed as a question. Examples from our recent work include:

How can we provide safe access to the beach while enhancing the beach environment and respecting the town's character and heritage?

How can our two teams work more effectively together to create a high quality customer experience where guests can enjoy the airport facilities and move easily and efficiently between flights, buses, taxis and car parking?

How do communities who are in conflict over use of natural resources develop a process for solution while remaining part of the groups in conflict?

A good question or statement framing a dilemma, in our view:

• Recognises the complexity inherent in the situation;

• Resonates with stakeholders and invites a creative response;

• Is something stakeholders actively want to find a solution for;

• Doesn't polarise or encourage confrontation;

• Is easily understood so stakeholders 'get it';

• Frames the challenge or dilemma in a way that emphasises mutual gains.

Our mission is to bring unlikely stakeholders together so they can learn about each other's perspectives and develop a working relationship that supports exploration of the dilemma. However, stepping back from the campaign rush towards a narrow solution can present a challenge. It takes leadership to stop the rush. Yet it remains a critical step to success. It takes a smart leader with the Power of 'Co' to tell the team to stop, think and plan how to identify and then invite all the right people to participate in a conversation.

Taking the time to define and appreciate the dilemma might seem like hard work, but once done it will fast track the co-creation of lasting solutions. And while it might seem infuriatingly slow at first, exploring different perspectives together provides a shared experience and establishes the building blocks of trust. It's this trust that will provide all parties with the confidence and energy to co-create an intelligent, creative, and enduring solution. People who don't trust those they are working with are much less likely to come up with something new and innovative. Trust leads to more positive relationships and a willingness to collaborate. In the end going slow will actually allow the process of finding a solution to go faster.

Taking the time to appreciate the dilemma also allows people to discover a common and safe space in which to start conversations and listen to each other. The key is to ensure that the process of defining the dilemma is a collaborative one that ensures everybody's perception of the problem is acknowledged as being valid.

Scenarios involving debate rather than dialogue are likely to produce argument. For example, when somebody in the group says, 'I think the problem looks like this', and someone else says, 'Well I don't agree with that, it's all a load of rubbish', a confrontational dynamic is created. Rather than arguing about different views, it's important that all stakeholders are acknowledged as having an interest in the dilemma.

Good facilitation by a skilled facilitator will help people work together and set the scene for the rest of the problem-solving activity. Getting all the perspectives on the table early only illuminates the complexity of the dilemma and the need to solve it in a different way.

This approach of exploring positions, interests and values early in a project to find common ground and build relationships is not altogether new. We have been using it in various situations relating to projects both large and small for many years.

When conducting a two-day facilitation program for a client several years ago, we spent the first day of the meeting just getting to know each other and understanding who was in the room. One particular individual was extremely frustrated with the approach, saying things like, 'We really need to get on with solving the problem, let's get on with it.' However, we held our ground, explaining that it was important to spend some time understanding all the different perspectives that were present. After that stage was concluded we absolutely breezed through the remainder of the activity. At the end of the second day that very same individual remarked, 'What a success! We never would have made progress if you hadn't taken the time on the first day to do that exercise.' However, this realisation was made only after the experience had concluded. To arrive at that point we had to endure significant resistance and tension about the time taken on seemingly irrelevant 'touchy-feely' time-wasting stuff. However, all involved ultimately recognised that it had been the steps in the process that helped get the group where it wanted to go.

Of course, there can be challenges. As we've noted before, there's frequently enormous pressure within sponsoring organisations to have certainty about both the problem and possible solutions before talking to stakeholders. It's a mindset driven by corporate pressures. After all, it's not easy for a technical expert or a senior manager to feel like an expert while saying, 'This is how we're experiencing this particular dilemma - what does it mean for you and how do you experience it?' Experts may feel less of an expert unless they have scoped the problem themselves and can propose a solution. Then they can adhere to the typical expert line of, 'If only you knew what I know, you would agree with me and we could implement my solution.' This is perhaps why water engineers find solutions in terms of pumps and pipes, why construction engineers find solutions in terms of building structures, why accountants find solutions in terms of reducing expenditure, increasing revenue or minimising tax, and why urban planners find solutions in planning policies, master plans and streetscapes.

For such experts, attempting to co-exist with a dilemma in a completely different way is a challenging but worthwhile exercise. Without the necessary pause to explore and share views on the dilemma there can be no widespread ownership of the definition of the dilemma. Consequently, stakeholders don't see themselves and their needs reflected in the dilemma definition. This increases the likelihood of resistance to any proposed solution. Indeed, while the proposed solution might resolve the dilemma the sponsoring organisation identifies, it may not address the aspects of stakeholder concern. This is something that may well cause the kind of unintended consequences we described in Chapter One. As a result, stakeholders may feel unacknowledged and decide to exercise their veto in active opposition. They may decide to provide oxygen to other political discontent or even inspire a new aspirant to stand for election on a one-issue platform. These are all foreseeable outcomes that can contribute to long-running project misery. Worse still, despite a solution being agreed upon, nothing happens.

It's also important to understand that there are no shortcuts in collaborative governance. We recently had an interesting experience with a government organisation that, keen to employ a collaborative process, commenced proceedings with what we would qualify as being Step Three. In effect, they attempted to design a collaborative process without taking the journey through Steps One and Two. This entailed many proposals, debates and discussions around who would be involved in the project team, who would actually be charged with finding solutions, who would be responsible for rendering technical advice, and who the approvers of the decision would be and how all the different groups would relate together in co-creating a solution. These issues proved extremely difficult to sort out as nobody actually had a clear idea about the scope of the problem they were trying to solve and the range of perspectives that might contribute it its complexity. Rather than first striving for clarity on problem scope with stakeholders, those who believed they fully understood the problem were preoccupied with how to set up a governance model that would include decision-makers and stakeholders, with provision for access to technical experts that satisfied political aspirations and policy-makers. Our concern was that this model didn't address how the groups would work together, how relationships and trust would be built and maintained and how consensus would be achieved in finding solutions.

Defining the Dilemma Together

If Step One is about committing to collaborate then Step Two is about the willingness to appreciate the dilemma together. This is where it all becomes real. This is where we actually get to experience the tension and the discomfort of stepping away from our preconceived solutions.

This links to the power paradox concept that we explored earlier. We might think of it this way: 'The less I focus on my dilemma and my solution, the more trusted and enabled I become. The more I focus on my dilemma and my solution, the more likely it is that energetic and passionate stakeholders, instead of contributing their energy to finding an enduring solution with me (for which I will get much credit) will try to limit my power and oppose my solution, which will reduce my likelihood of eventual success.'

For leaders and decision-makers, the challenge is to cease being powerful around their preferred solution. It's about allowing everyone time, space and the opportunity to describe the problem in their terms and encouraging stakeholders to recognise that the dilemma itself will include a technical aspect, a financial aspect, a social aspect, a cultural aspect, an environmental aspect, as well as whatever aspect their perspective entails. As such, it's important to encourage stakeholders to share and explore all aspects of the problem rather than merely concentrating on the one that they're familiar with. Hearing someone talk with certainty about things that others may lack knowledge of can be very comforting.

All this effort can be seen as being a key investment, and this phase of the problem-solving process is the crucial time to make that investment. Although in many cases there may be a desire within the sponsoring organisation to engage in 'campaign rush' or the push to arrive at a position or decision as quickly as possible, finding a solution together is not likely to flow easily if the exact nature of the problem isn't precisely defined, understood and appreciated at the outset. Furthermore, failing to implement this step is likely to lead to long-term problems and complexities that may extract a significant toll.

An Example of the Challenge of Going Slow to Go Fast

In Chapter Three we looked at the case of a state government body that had purchased a parcel of land in expectation that it would be used for a freeway development. They then decided that the political landscape had changed and they no longer needed it. But governmental policy required the department to scope the problem and define what they saw as the solution before funds could be allocated to implementing any subsequent initiative. Their definition of the problem was their need to use the funds currently invested in the land for other road projects. Therefore, they needed a strategy for selling the land at the best possible price.

This highlights one of the significant institutional challenges that may arise when it comes to gaining an appreciation of the dilemma. In this situation, it's very hard to attract funding for a project that involves working together to understand the dilemma. Government backers want to know the outcome before they commit funds. They want to know how the funds will be spent and what benefits will be generated. To work within these guidelines, the road authority's strategy became: produce a master plan for the area in question - the master plan being the solution. Then, persuade people that this is necessary while highlighting benefits such as better amenities for different public areas as well as some new developments. However, because the tract of land had long been used by people for activities like bicycle and horse riding, rumours of land development and resulting loss of leisure space led to community concern and negative reaction.

How different would the conversation have been if the road authority had first approached local government, relevant stakeholders and community groups and said: 'Our dilemma is that we have this land we don't need anymore and it's our responsibility to get a financial return. We recognise that you are stakeholders in how this land is used so please come and explore this dilemma with us and help us solve it.' But instead of engaging with the community to arrive at a dilemma appreciation that embraced its true complexity, the authority felt they had no alternative but to consult with the community about a draft master plan concept as a solution, even though they recognised that this was likely to create opposition and antagonism.

For some stakeholders, seeing that the dilemma-defining process is inclusive of their individual concerns may well be enough for them to feel satisfied and valued. They may then be quite happy to accommodate other concerns or perspectives. Perhaps their only commitment to the process centres on making sure that any solution will solve their part of that dilemma. If they're happy with the problem definition and trust that their part of it will be solved, then they may not want to participate in any other part of the process.

We've already spoken about the huge amounts of discretionary energy that people have to solve an issue they feel passionate about. This is the opportunity to tap into and utilise it. You can invite them in to use the energy to work together, or they will use their energy to push for their own solution. If they're not invited in they're likely to work against you. We know from experience that if groups are not encouraged to take part in the conversation they will create their own forums to solve the problem as they see it. That might translate to holding a project up or stopping it altogether. Inviting them in early creates the opportunity to have a wider conversation.

Painting the Picture – What Success Looks Like
Appreciating the dilemma is an extremely important stage. But when it comes to achieving a commitment from stakeholders to collaborate, arriving at a definition of what success actually looks like will play just as big a part. When we ask what success looks like (or what matters to stakeholders about a solution), we are really asking what needs to happen, what needs to eventuate, what boxes need to be ticked in order for the problem to be deemed solved? Visualising this picture will play a big role in determining

the shape of the subsequent decision-making process.

Painting a picture of success can be another way of streamlining and simplifying the process of co-creating a solution. Understanding what a 'good' solution looks like sometimes narrows down possible solution options, especially if none of them appear to satisfy the picture of success that stakeholders have agreed is necessary.

Another way of putting it is that to be able to identify the best solution from a range of options requires agreement on 'decision criteria'. While decision criteria are featured in most literature covering decision-making, our experience tells us that many people find the whole concept quite difficult.

When asked to help a client design an engagement process, it has been our approach for many years to focus attention on engaging stakeholders and communities to participate in establishing principles or values that need to be visible in the final solution. For example, we have worked frequently in situations where the required decision has related to the placement of a piece of infrastructure such as a wastewater treatment plant, a water treatment plant, a solid waste dump, an electricity sub-station, transmission lines, wind farms, a stock effluent management facility or even a dam or pipeline.

Rather than get into debates, discussions and arguments about whether it should be Site A, B or C, or none of them, which generally create much heat and not much light, we have found it more effective to start with the 'givens' of the piece of infrastructure. That is, parameters such as size, shape, height, visibility, noise, dust, litter, vibrations, timing of operations, movements in and out, odour, and so on. We then take members of the affected community to look at a similar piece of infrastructure in another location and talk to residents there. When they understand the nature of what is to be built, they are then in a position to establish relevant local criteria for their site.

As a result, the community can collaborate with the purpose of setting criteria for positioning a wastewater treatment plant. Such criteria may include:

- An appropriate sized site with an existing buffer zone of a certain size around it that will be zoned to exclude residential buildings in future.

- A site that is sufficiently close to the residences it will serve so that sewage can be piped to the plant as energy efficiently as possible.

- A site that allows for wastewater to be piped directly from the plant to, and used beneficially for, irrigation of pastures, golf courses, parks and gardens or disposed of into suitable water bodies in times of wet weather.

- A site where trees and shrubs screen the plant from sight.

Additional local criteria might also be added as a result of particular local needs. If these criteria are co-created by the community prior to any potential sites being identified, then as a feasibility study is undertaken, the engineers can discount sites that don't meet the criteria and produce a short list of options. A preferred site can then be selected by application of the community's criteria.

Working with clients to establish useful criteria against which to evaluate options has often been challenging. In helping practitioners and project managers to assess the usefulness of the criteria they develop we have developed this checklist. A set of useful criteria should:
- reflect shared stakeholder interests and issues;
- invite a creative and enthusiastic response from stakeholders;
- acknowledge the tension inherent in the dilemma in a positive way;
- be easily understood;
- emphasise the potential for mutual gains; i.e. reflect the diversity of what matters to stakeholders.

A set of criteria for the improvements on the main street of the Victorian country town mentioned earlier might have included the following:

- maintain shade during summer months;
- allow easy access to and along pavements for wheel chairs, prams and cycles;
- minimise hazards for pedestrians which cause trips and falls;
- facilitate easy 45° angle car parking for shoppers and visitors;
- minimise changes to the streetscape;
- include the replacement of any tree removed with a sapling of an appropriate species.

An example of the challenge some people find in understanding the difference between decision-criteria and solutions occurred when we were working with a local Council who needed to make a decision about a local aquatic centre.

We had suggested to Councillors that the community could most usefully be engaged in establishing success factors for the new centre; that is, the criteria that the final design for the centre had to meet. In this case, stakeholders met to consider the opportunities that the new centre could provide.

When asked what mattered to them about the new centre, many people said that it must contain a 50-metre pool. If it didn't, the new aquatic centre wouldn't be a success. To us, a 50-metre pool looked like part of the solution rather than a decision criterion, so we tried to tease out why they wanted a 50-metre pool. That is, what was it about a 50-metre pool that was so important? Or why did a 50-metre pool matter so much to them? At that point things became quite fuzzy and obscured because the distinction between criteria and solutions wasn't clear to them.

The closest we got was to establish that the new aquatic centre was about providing exercise opportunities for a wide range of users including professional swimmers. Therefore, the criteria was a pool of a length that would enable professional training, that is, 50 metres.

In this case, our attempt to collaborate on appropriate criteria failed, either because we were unable to explain the concept of criteria effectively or because the swimming fraternity had fixed its position on a 50-metre pool and was unable to let go.

This situation confirmed for us how important it is for decision criteria to be established before any attempt is made to generate options. If stakeholders already hold a firm position that a particular option is the only solution they will support, they are likely to try and establish criteria that will support the selection of that particular option. In other words, the criteria established will not be objective and reflect the needs of all stakeholders.

During Step Two of the Collaborative Governance process we have found that spending time to explore what matters to stakeholders in relation to a solution before ascertaining what that solution needs to address in order to solve the dilemma and avoid unintended consequences is another exercise that builds understanding of different perspectives and encourages conversations about things that matter.

Such conversations also expose areas of ignorance among stakeholders about aspects of the dilemma and potential solutions – something that allows some shared research and information gathering by stakeholders. This is another activity that builds relationships and trust.

Determining what success looks like drives creativity and innovation. It creates a platform for progress because it acknowledges the fact that all interests, needs and aspirations must be explored and addressed. It encourages participants to ask themselves, 'How clever can we be in taking all this into account?'

Defining success early in the collaborative process also reduces polarisation and avoids having a bunch of things on a wish list, which is often how people will view a solution. It makes people more open to finding solutions and perhaps modifying their own ideas to incorporate others.

If a definition of success can be agreed upon, it's not such a stretch to assume that agreement on the best possible solution can also be reached. Additionally, the process also establishes a strong likelihood that whatever solution emerges will stick because stakeholders have worked together to create the characteristics (the success picture) before getting into possible solutions.

Things to Ponder

Having a conversation about the nature of dilemmas is not a simple thing to do. We've outlined a number of the challenges in this chapter, but there are a number of other stumbling blocks to open conversation as well.

These can present in the form of subjects or issues deemed controversial, taboo, or simply off limits. For example, how do you have a conversation that may involve the disclosure of politically or commercially sensitive information?

How do you have a discussion where some of the prevailing issues are widely seen as un-discussable, such as race or religion? And how do you have a conversation where one party may be unwilling to share certain information because it weakens their own position?

An organisation can find collaboration challenging if part of the dilemma is the legacy of their poor past performance. We have been part of processes where less than perfect legacies have been difficult to discuss. These are hard questions, but important to consider. Full and frank appreciation of a dilemma may depend on it.

Another significant challenge to openness and transparency is the role of the media and the relationships organisations have with various news organisations. Many Councillors complain to us about local journalists who keep giving them a hard time. This is a part of the dilemma from a Council perspective. How do they invite everyone in to an uncertain question when just having the conversation means copping a beating by the press?

We have found that thinking more appreciatively about the media is a good strategy. Approaching a journalist or a news editor proactively as a potential ally, explaining the collaborative approach and seeking their support in communicating the process to their audience has been successful for us. In a recent project we actually had an editor offer to put a map insert into his paper to explain the options, as he believed his community needed good information.

Official spokespeople find it a challenge to report openly, accurately and honestly when they know that whatever they say will be negatively presented the next day in the media. Former Victorian Police Commissioner Christine Nixon tells of how, after a media conference or a media interview, she would approach the news reports with a sinking feeling in anticipation of their possible interpretation of the situation. With one bad piece of press having the potential to change the way somebody's leadership is perceived, this can have a big impact on a leader's willingness to take on the risk of a new approach to finding a solution to a very real and complex dilemma.

Media and political issues can be showstoppers when it only takes one stakeholder to provide a negative view to the media to blast a whole collaborative process out of the water.

Courage and Smart Leadership
The whole concept of dilemma appreciation relates back to the issue of smart leadership. While it's often the case that leaders see themselves as having to come up with all the answers, a smart leader assumes the role of convener - the person who brings together issues, interests and values. The leader's role in this instance is to bring people together for that conversation on the understanding that it builds the foundation from which governance and solutions can be created.

In short, a smart leader will realise that it's not up to them to have all the answers, just to provide the crucible from which good solutions can emerge.

But as we've already examined, opting to take such an approach can be risky. The challenge is in branding smart leadership as both practical and powerful. Reframing can be useful here. Governments and organisations need to reframe the concept of engaging in collaborative processes as a demonstration of effective and practical leadership.

To make it work leaders have to be able to articulate what they're doing. Because it's much easier for people outside the process to knock it than to understand it, the leader as facilitator must be able to explain their course of action in a way that addresses community fears and media criticism and demonstrates the participatory role of stakeholders in dilemma-solving.

A bold, courageous leader is one who says, 'This is how we see it, which may be a narrow view. We need a wider stakeholder perspective in order for us all to have a better idea about the scope and complexity of this issue so we can find solutions together.'

By the end of Step Two, it's necessary for stakeholders and the sponsoring organisation to agree on the scope of the dilemma and what matters about its solution before progressing to Step Three.

This is another necessary pre-condition for successful collaboration. The decision-makers, with the support of the collaborative governance team, will have commenced a partnership with their stakeholders and appreciate what each stakeholder will bring to the collaborative process. Together they will have defined the dilemma in all its complexities and have explored what matters to each stakeholder about its solution.

Key Learnings from Chapter 5

- Taking time to clarify and define the dilemma so that it includes all the perspectives will fast track the solutions

- Working on defining the dilemma together build relationships and trust

- Determining what success looks like creates a platform for progress and simplifies finding the best possible solution

Chapter 6

Step Three – Co-Designing the Process

"If you're not at the table, you're probably on the menu"

A comment overheard at an IAP2 conference

Co-design process by sharing process options, considering context and resources and co-creating an appropriate and workable governance structure and engagement process.

In Chapter Five we examined the importance of defining the dilemma in conjunction with stakeholders and decision-makers. Along the way we demonstrated how this initiative not only creates a positive working environment in which to solve a complex dilemma, but also ensures that the definition of the dilemma reflects all its complexities and challenges. With a clear picture now in place, it's time to instigate the all-important journey from dilemma to solution, using a framework that will ultimately result in the co-creation and implementation of an enduring outcome. Just what that journey will look like, who its participants will be, and what methodology will influence decision-making as proceedings unfold are all important considerations as we undertake Step Three.

It's here that stakeholders start to explore the role of collaboration as part of decision-making. It's here that the reasoning behind the term Collaborative Governance becomes clearer.

The sponsoring organisation and the stakeholders who have indicated a willingness to collaborate need to explore:-

- what the governance structure for the process will look like;
- who needs to be part of the collaboration;
- who will be outside it but nonetheless constantly informed of what the collaborators are doing;
- who will take the outcome of the collaboration forward.

The governance (or decision-making) structure will almost certainly be different for each collaborative decision-making process.

The time to design a collaborative decision-making structure is when:-

- the sponsoring organisation has made a genuine commitment to collaboration;
- the value that stakeholders can add to the process has been explored through an appreciative stakeholder analysis;
- the true nature and scope of the dilemma has been agreed;as a result of working together, positive relationships and trust are starting to develop between the potential collaborators and there is a shared willingness to explore the decision-making process.

If a governance structure is decided upon prior to these outcomes (as was the case in an example mentioned in Chapter Five), there is a risk that collaborators will want to revisit it once the process begins.

When stakeholders are presented with a governance structure at the time they are invited in (often in the form of a diagram with lines, boxes and arrows on paper), they will make inferences about how that diagram will translate into working relationships, roles and responsibilities.

However, such a diagram cannot describe relationships between different stakeholder groups encompassing bureaucrats, politicians, technical experts, businesses and communities. Worse, different people will interpret such diagrams quite differently and may enter the collaboration with a range of unacknowledged and unchallenged assumptions.

When stakeholders don't have an opportunity to be part of the development of the decision-making process or their role within it, they may well ask how truly collaborative the process will be. If an important component is not decided collaboratively, they may conclude that the promise of collaboration is not genuine. As a result, they may then refuse to participate and, when a solution is agreed upon by the remaining collaborators, exercise their veto, or worse, undermine or obstruct its implementation.

Sharing Options

What governance structures will work best for a particular collaboration? This is an important question. There is a risk that the co-designers won't think broadly enough and will simply focus on structures, methods or techniques for engagement and decision-making that have proven effective in the past. The belief seems to be that if a certain governance structure has worked for solving a problem before, then replicating it must surely be a good idea. In reality, this is an approach that seldom works, simply because: every context is different; today's decision-makers will face different constraints and opportunities; the stakeholders will almost certainly have different expectations. Therefore, any governance structure will need to reflect those differences and be tailored to suit. Previous models may be too complicated for a given context. Or they may be too simple. Either way, the resulting fit will be anything but perfect.

The completion of Step Two opens up a new set of questions for the collaboration, starting with: what kind of governance structure options are there and how will we select the 'right' one for our collaborative process?

It's interesting to note that a Google search of 'governance structure' will produce 16 pages of diagrams depicting different governance structure models, with 24 options on each page. That makes 384 different diagrams, each an illustration of an actual governance structure that has been utilised at some point by an organisation or project team. So there is no shortage of options.

Whether your governance structure is subsequently represented as a triangle, a solar system, a hub and spokes, an organisational chart or something more organic, the important questions for decision-makers and stakeholders to consider together include:
- Who has the ultimate mandate and authority to approve any recommendations made by collaborators?
- Who has given them their authority and can it be taken away before the end of the collaboration?
- How ready are those with the authority to support the collaborative

process?

- Are they bound to endorse any consensual decision made by the collaborators or can they ignore it, set it aside or openly disagree with it?
- Who is in the collaborative group and whom does it represent?
- Are there stakeholders outside the group who would like to be inside, and who decides?
- What does collaboration mean to both the collaborators and those who approve their recommendations?
- How are decisions made within the collaborative group? Must all decisions be made by consensus or can decisions be made that some stakeholders actively disagree with, and who decides?
- Who provides the budget for the collaboration and who decides what is needed?
- Do all the stakeholders have the same role and the same level of influence on decisions?
- Are there subgroups within the collaborative group and if so, what is their role?
- Are there other groups (external to the collaboration) that need to understand and approve the collaborators' work?
- Will specialist technical expertise be required by the collaborators? Who decides and who will provide it?
- Whose technical experts are going to be trusted and relied upon?
- What happens if there are technical experts who don't agree?
- What other data or information needs to be researched or collected?
- Who is going to collect it and to whom will it be given?
- How much time will be allowed for the collaboration? Will it be enough for collaborators to do their work?
- Will collaborators be reimbursed for their time?
- How will the outcomes of the collaboration be taken forward?

The resulting collaborative structure will depend on the answers to these and other questions.

Keep It Simple
It's a maxim that applies to many things. Governance structures designed

to support the co-creation of solutions are certainly no exception. Making something unnecessarily complicated is risky. If stakeholders and decision-makers are confused by the number of groups, the roles they play, who approves what, who is in and who is out, then the collaborative process is likely to lose energy and focus and may ultimately fail. When people are asked to implement a process that is easy to understand (be it either a decision-making or engagement process), they're more likely to accept it.

A good example is a project we worked on in regional New South Wales.

In order to encourage collaboration with a local community, the sponsoring organisation decided to establish an advisory group. In our experience, advisory groups seem to pop up all over the place. 'We have to work with the community therefore we should establish an advisory group' seems to be a default position, possibly because the technique is often supported, or required, by state governments in sensitive situations. In this case, we questioned whether this was the appropriate structure for engaging the community in the dilemma the company was trying to solve. We suggested that, rather than establishing an advisory group, it would be more effective to first engage the stakeholders in defining the dilemma.

In response, the company actually stepped back to give themselves and their stakeholders more time to create confidence in working together. They started two processes simultaneously. They first clarified their version of the dilemma and asked for other perspectives.

The second involved asking questions about what governance structure would encourage stakeholders to participate and give them confidence in their role in developing a solution. The questions covered many areas, including the makeup of those involved, their roles and responsibilities, and how stakeholders might work with the company in the quest to arrive at a solution.

Rather than choosing simply to impose a problem and a process, the smart leaders recognised the importance of ascertaining whether more could be done to make working together effective and valuable.

Resisting Temptation

It's important to realise that imposing governance structures on stakeholders is just as risky as imposing a solution. It is also just as tempting, especially if favoured structures, techniques or process designs have yielded good outcomes in the past.

One particular instance of this occurred two decades ago when a particularly emotional drama was being played out in the northern New South Wales coastal town of Coffs Harbour. The Council of the day was overseeing unprecedented growth and recognised that they needed additional sewerage infrastructure to reduce the strain on failing old sewage pipes and accommodate ongoing coastal development.

This meant finding ways of disposing of treated waste water, which on the coast inevitably meant either exploring new and innovative but as yet unproven ways to re-use it for land irrigation or release it into the ocean. There was an emotional public reaction to both options, which resulted in a two-year moratorium on ocean sewer outfalls of any kind in NSW as well as keen interest in potential safe uses of highly treated waste water.

As part of the project decision-making process, Council established an Inter-Departmental Committee (IDC), which involved regular meetings of members from all relevant State Government departments. The aim of the committee was to provide a "whole of government" approach to assessing potential solutions before adoption by Council.

Some two years later a similar situation arose in another coastal town, and those with the responsibility for finding a solution immediately requested their own "IDC". It seemed to us that the desire came more from "wanting what they had" rather than from a clear idea of what role an IDC could play in solving their similar but not identical local issue.

Collaboration on an agreed structure that all stakeholders own and understand is a much more respectful and in our view robust approach than convincing stakeholders that a pre-determined structure should be adopted. Collaborative Governance only works if a respectful, appreciative and deliberative approach is continued right through all the five steps.

The important thing for leaders to remember is that this doesn't mean giving up any of their traditional control over the decision-making process or the eventual outcome. It means using smart power to deliver stronger and more sustainable outcomes for their organisation because the collaborative outcomes stick.

Think about it for a moment. In the world of complex issues, people tend to be vexed. They tend to have polarised perspectives. They gather with those who think the same, reinforcing and strengthening their positions. They're often upset, angry and frustrated.

Consequently, the environment is highly charged and difficult. Attempting to impose process (however good it might be) is riskier in these high-energy situations, as suspicions abound about whose agenda is being pushed.

When we were involved in the Sydney Airport Master Plan one of the things that we were adamant about was not starting any process of collaboration until there was corporate and political agreement on a question that might be put to a community panel. And while it took nine months to get agreement on what that question would be, it was a very important piece of the design.

Until we knew what the panel had to address, we couldn't go any further. That episode served to demonstrate that sometimes you have to go to extravagant lengths to build confidence by allowing people to create a process for themselves so they own it and can commit to and participate in it. Only then will they believe that the process is fair and robust.

A Dilemma for Leaders

Some leaders and organisations are reluctant to adopt this approach. They think that decisions are something they make, and when required by law to consult on a proposed decision, they see consultation as something that is done by them to their stakeholders.

In New Zealand, the phrases "the draft will go out for consultation next week", or "the four-week consultation period will start on Monday following the launch of the draft document" are heard regularly.

This reflects a typical consultation process where the sponsoring organisation has done all the hard work in creating the plan or document describing what the organisation intends to do.

The intent of the consultation is to give informed and articulate people an opportunity to read and respond to the document with comments or questions within the specified time. These will be acknowledged formally before the final document is released. This formal, regulated activity may have its uses for simple or even complicated problems that government and non-government organisations need to find solutions to. However, we contend that this approach is completely unhelpful as a response to complex or controversial dilemmas.

But for decision-makers who are familiar and comfortable with the familiar formal consultation processes, the idea of engaging or collaborating differently could be seen as convoluted, time-consuming, nebulous and completely unnecessary. Perhaps they haven't experienced the power and energy that can be harnessed in solving a really complex and controversial dilemma together.

Is there an inherent dilemma here? Should the question be: *"Under what circumstances is it more effective for leaders and stakeholders in a problem or dilemma to participate together in creative solution-making, and what would the benefits be?"* Perhaps that is a useful conversation to have as a precursor to collaboration.

Considering context and resources
We have discussed a range of contexts in which collaboration may be

considered. The kind of problem that has arisen, its complexity and the range of stakeholders and positions on its solution is one context we have explored.

Community interest in the decision, as well as the associated collective capacity to participate in a different approach to solving complex dilemmas, is another. As such, it is important to find out as much as possible about the community of interest, to listen to its stories, to understand what brings it together and what polarises it before stepping into a collaborative process. Has there been a history of conflict around this dilemma? What attempts have been made to solve it in the past, and how resilient has the community been in dealing with success and failure? How important is this problem to the functioning of this community? Is the community a local one, a regional one, a national one, or an international one?

An important context may be in the range of worldviews within a community of interest. Indeed, we recently found ourselves confronting two radically different worldviews around environmental issues in New Zealand. On one hand a scientific, reductionist worldview seemed to be saying, 'We can only solve this problem using science. It is beneficial to understand the problem by pulling it apart and working out which bits to fix, applying the solution and then putting everything back together.' Those with an alternative worldview struggled with this. 'Everything is interdependent,' they said. 'If you pull something apart you destroy it.

When we apply a solution in one place, everything around it is affected. We and our communities are integral parts of the natural world, not separate from it.'

How can you work together across those two worldviews? The reality is that you won't change a person's perspective by telling them they've got it wrong. The process of working together must allow different worldviews to find their own way into a solution that everyone can live with.

This is not simple, and it's not about finding the best and easiest way that we all agree with. Rather, it's about understanding people's belief systems, their way of identifying fairness and equity, and their ability to work and share with people who have a different worldview. It's acknowledging that neither viewpoint is right or wrong, but merely different, and that curiosity regarding the other worldview is more useful than rejection.

Skills and resources within a community of interest will also affect its capacity and willingness to collaborate. With this in mind, a skills audit may be a valuable way of finding out the extent of skills and knowledge about the dilemma and its many perspectives. Who are the people who lead the community and what skills can they bring? Who is trusted and respected and are they willing to get involved? Is there a particular group with specialist knowledge that might be helpful? How cohesive is a particular community and what levels of trust exist between groups? Are there high or low levels of social capital?

Co-Designing the Process

So, how might we harness the energy, skill and knowledge within the community of interest to co-design a process? The Appreciative Inquiry method is an extremely useful way of exploring the nature of stakeholders' best experiences and revealing the aspects that engender confidence in decision-making. This can be ascertained by conducting a simple appreciative interview exercise to draw out the stories or examples of when people have had confidence in a process.

From this, we can determine some key pre-requisites. What do we need to pay attention to? What are the factors that create confidence? What would contribute to a good process? That kind of discovery process, undertaken through Appreciative Inquiry, can be incredibly useful in saying, 'Well we've had experience of what gives us confidence – let's do more of that.

Let's actually draw on those stories to help design a process we believe is not outside of our experience and try to build on that.' This is a respectful way of going about that goal.

As indicated at the start of Chapter Four, a Collaborative Governance process starts with the decision-makers' willingness to commit to collaboration. The first questions in the list provided earlier in this chapter will almost certainly have been explored as part of Step One.

The Governance Structure

The formulation of a governance structure will start with those who have the ultimate mandate and authority to solve the problem, both from an organisational and an individual perspective.

Their commitment to collaboration is a necessary pre-requisite to a collaborative process. Those possessing the mandate and authority will constitute the apex of the pyramid, the centre of the solar system, the top of the organisational chart, the hub of the wheel or the heart of the system.

The next part of establishing the governance structure will depend on the answers to questions about the roles of the collaborators, including:

• Who is in the collaborative group and whom does it represent?

• What does collaboration mean to both the collaborators and those who approve their recommendations?

• How are decisions made within the collaborative group - must all decisions be made by consensus or can decisions be made that some stakeholders actively disagree with, and who decides?

• Do all the stakeholders have the same role and the same level of influence on decisions?

• Are there subgroups within the collaborative group and if so, what is their role?

Some of these questions will have been addressed in Step Two during the process of identifying and recruiting stakeholders into the collaborative governance process and undertaking an Appreciative Stakeholder Analysis.

Potential collaborators will have been asking for answers to these questions as they decide whether solving this dilemma through a collaborative process is a good use of their own personal and organisational time. For them to accept a collaborative role, they need to have confidence that the work they do will genuinely influence the leaders involved and contribute to an enduring solution.

The Process Documented

Collaborators need to develop their own *Statement of Collaborative Intent* that integrates with the *Statement of Collaborative Intent* signed by the ultimate decision-maker at the end of Step One.

This Statement will include a Terms of Reference, a set of principles or a Memorandum of Understanding that sets out clearly the way the collaborators agree to work together.

It needs to be created and signed off by the collaborators themselves and agreed upon by the ultimate decision-makers.

This statement may also include relevant operational commitments such as:

- how and by whom the overall project will be managed.
- the level of administrative support the collaborators will be provided with and by whom;
- the time, money and personnel resources available to them;
- how and by whom their meetings will be facilitated;
- who will provide any technical information or advice they will need throughout the collaboration.

Relationships with stakeholders external to the collaborations will also need to be addressed in the Statement, particularly the way the collaborators will represent the views of their constituent organisations within the collaboration and keep them informed on the collaboration's progress.

The statement needs to make it very clear how the agreed solutions from the collaborative governance process will be taken forward to the ultimate decision-makers at the end of Step Four.

The governance structure and the relationships between collaborators, facilitator or collaborative guide, technical experts, government agency staff, other stakeholders who are not collaborators as well as the wider communities of interest and the decision-makers, will emerge from these conversations and are likely to become part of the Statement of Collaborative Intent.

The co-definition of the dilemma and what matters to stakeholders about its solution (which represented the endpoint of Step Two), may also be included for clarity.

The Size of Collaborating Groups
Another important aspect of collaborative structuring relates to the actual size of the group involved. After all, just how many people can work together effectively? Once again, there are no easy answers, just some guidelines to help identify what will work best in different situations.

In his article entitled "Innovating" (in which he discusses the distinction between Collaboration and the other 'C' words: co-operation, co-ordination and communication), Leo Denise makes it clear that he believes collaboration "is not about agreement. It is about creation." Collaboration, according to Denise, is about using information to create something new, to seek divergent insights, to thrive on difference and to ignite the sparks of dissent. Collaborative processes are established to solve problems, develop new understandings and design new products.

Because of these particular aspects, Denise suggests that they begin with just a few people of different experiences and viewpoints. He contends that the only reason for adding more people is for the injection of some new and essential element.

John Paul Lederach suggests that problems are solved when improbable sets of people are brought together - people who think differently and have different and even opposing views. He likens a collaborative process to a particular soup where, paradoxically, every bean keeps its flavor while a brand new taste is created.

Alastair Bisley, the chair of the Land and Water Forum in New Zealand, commenced his collaborative process by inviting as many stakeholders as he could identify. What's more, he encouraged them to send their most senior representatives.

He started with a group of around 60 who became a Plenary Group, and from this a Small Group was identified. In a speech given in January 2011, Alastair indicated that *"the participants in the Small Group devoted on average one third of their time to the Land and Water Forum – and that is on top of their day jobs. They also made a large and generous investment of energy … in this process and its outcomes."*

Over the years, we at Twyfords have used a broad range of collaborative techniques including Citizens' Juries Community Panels and deliberative forums of various kinds. As a general rule, we consider groups of between 12 and 20 people to be effective for the purposes of working together for a reasonably lengthy period to deliberate about complex dilemmas and create enduring solutions.

We have also found it highly beneficial to provide any group with early opportunities to get to know each other, to tell stories, to challenge each other about the dilemma, to go and look at things together, to eat together and have conversations about the way they want to work together before starting the process of solution co-creation.

At this point, it's worth considering how the wisdom of non-aligned stakeholders who have no particular position on the dilemma may be accessed. Such people have much to offer if they are given the chance to become informed, are given time to understand the issues and explore perspectives and then deliberate together to find a solution.

Sometimes obvious stakeholders are so vested in their positions and so loud in their advocacy for a particular position that leaders see them as dangerous participants in any potential collaboration. Sometimes those stakeholders are unwilling to participate in a collaborative process because they believe it will compromise them in the minds of their colleagues and fellow activists.

Such stakeholders may never agree on a solution. However, they may agree to a process that allows non-aligned citizens to hear the arguments from all sides, deliberate and arrive at a recommendation. They may support a process that addresses what is accepted as a vexed and complex dilemma that needs to be solved, that listens to and appreciates different interests and perspectives, that is demonstrably fair, and leads to a decision made by a group of people without any personal interest in the outcome. They may want the opportunity of putting their case to this randomly selected, informed and deliberative group to make sure their arguments and passions are considered in the decision-making process.

They may want assurances that the non-aligned citizens will objectively assess the information and have time to deliberate effectively. We have found that collaborative processes such as Citizens' Juries, Community Panels and Deliberative Forums, or any others where all or some of the participants are randomly selected can provide sufficient confidence for the activists on all sides to agree to accept the solutions or recommendations that come from within them.

The strength of the Collaborative Governance process centres on achieving stakeholder buy-in and using their energy and enthusiasm to design a process and build support for the deliberative element of collaboration.

Whatever the size the collaborative group or the process and governance structure in play, there will be people who choose not to be part of the collaboration but who are still very interested in both the process and the outcome.

The question thus becomes: How do these stakeholders stay involved?

How do we create effective communications between the collaborators, the decision-makers and the broader stakeholder group so that we avoid there being any surprises once the collaborators come to their recommendations?

Effective communication will be required. A spokesperson for the collaboration may need to be appointed. Target groups may need to be identified including those who need to be kept informed of progress, those who want to provide information to the collaboration, and those who can act as critical reviewers or advisers. Communication tools need to be identified or developed and resources provided. What is important is ensuring a broad understanding of the process and its progress as well as a 'no surprises' outcome.

Co-Design that Encourages Stakeholders to Participate Freely
Sometimes legislation will compel a government body to undertake public meetings and a submission process with a view to reaching a final decision. As such, some of the process design elements are already prescribed within legislated frameworks.

We have found that there is both potential to influence those who write legislation, regulations or guidelines to design them in such a way that allows some space for creative process design as well as space for innovation and creativity within such frameworks.

Another challenge we have worked hard at addressing occurs when clients or stakeholders believe that only people who understand and support a particular view should participate in a collaborative process.

They believe that participants must be 100 percent committed to the process of finding a solution and be prepared to defend the process, or not be in it.

We recommend that our clients do not try to prevent stakeholders from protesting or getting involved outside the process. People have a democratic right to do so and their participation in a collaborative process should not preclude them from lobbying or pushing a particular case.

Indeed, a process may even become endangered if collaborators are not constantly curious about stakeholders with different views or are unable to provide clear reasons and evidence for their own views. Collaboration means balancing advocacy (which entails communicating one's own views clearly and with reasons) with inquiry (which entails seeking to understand the views of others, no matter how different). We are confident that the process will be better for accommodating the broadest possible range of opinions.

The experience with coal seam gas exploration and associated community opposition in eastern Australia indicates how important this approach can be. While communities are saying, "We are locking the gate because we just don't want you here," some people are taking up opportunities to maintain respectful conversations without being issued with requests to change their views.

As long as they're not told they have to open the gate, people will step into these conversations and can be encouraged to discuss whether they would be prepared to step into any kind of collaborative process with a governance structure they could co-design. The need and the desire to solve a dilemma sometimes make such conversations possible.

The extent to which participants are willing to work together to co-design the process will depend to some degree on how well trust has been established in the earlier stages. If people don't step into co-designing a process, chances are this is because they're not comfortable about a sponsor's commitment to collaborate or they are not confident that the prevailing dilemma has been defined to their satisfaction.

If resistance is a factor, it's probably worth going back to ascertain whether enough trust and credibility has in fact been established for others to collaborate on designing a process. In these instances, being honest enough to say, 'It looks like we don't understand the dilemma well enough to proceed through this process – let's stop and take the time to go back', can ultimately reap the necessary dividends.

When to Make the Investment

Clients often ask us how they should decide when a collaborative process is desirable. We believe that the projects where collaborative processes can add the most value are those entailing a high risk of community outrage and serious long-term damage to an organisation's credibility. When decisions that will have a negative impact on stakeholders are made secretly behind closed doors and then announced and hotly defended, the organisation loses credibility.

Where the organisation is accused of telling lies and hiding information from communities, leaders sometimes find themselves staring into an abyss of community anger and facing a media disaster from which it may take years to recover. When leaders are discovered colluding together for their own benefit at the expense of individuals and communities who can't fight back, their reputations may be irreparably damaged. These situations can be extremely costly in terms of the loss of trust that ensues. One client even referred to such an instance as "17 years of misery" – a term that related to the whole life of a project that was approved by government but hated by the community.

There can be no doubt that there are situations where making a sound early investment in sharing the dilemma with local communities represents fundamental value for money. Asking open and respectful questions like, "How can we conserve this native forest while still giving local communities the right to use the resource and ensure the livelihood of local communities?" is much more likely to start exploratory conversations, produce energy to co-design a decision-making process, and enable the co-creation of innovative solutions for shared implementation.

But as well as these obvious situations (to us at least), if we look at typical project budgets and the areas where expenditure is traditionally allocated, we are pretty sure that available funds are mostly spent on things like planning and design and the acquisition of approvals or resource consents. This may even involve defending the project in the Environment Court and then implementing the decision.

We do not often observe funds being allocated for risk assessment, particularly the risk associated with not inviting stakeholders into the project right from the start. But a relatively small upfront investment in a Collaborative Governance process that invites the public in, shares the dilemma, seeks an understanding of it from the community's perspective and then offers the opportunity to solve it together can yield many invaluable long-term benefits.

In doing our community engagement work over the last 20 years, we have always recommended to clients that they need to allocate a budget for engaging communities that is commensurate with the risks involved should their project or policy create long-term toxic relationships or trigger the necessity to spend unbudgeted funds on backing and filling when things go wrong and communities become outraged.

Our advice has always been to spend 60% of any engagement budget in the planning stages when the project is nothing more than lines on paper.

In our Collaborative Governance work we recognise that an investment in Steps One, Two and Three will provide significant dividends. During these steps the decision-makers make a decision about the value of collaborative process, work with stakeholders to co-define the dilemma and also co-design the decision-making and governance structure.

While much work still has to be done in Steps Four and Five, the foundation elements of trust and shared understanding are in place, which means it is possible to fast-track that work.

Opting not to invest in these early stages can have dire consequences. Indeed, stories abound where projects go way over time and budget because of delays caused by community outrage, or where organisations have paid exorbitant legal fees and engaged in lengthy, unpleasant court battles, sometimes never to achieve their desired outcome. Similar stories exist where decisions were made that made very little sense to anyone other than to the narrow focused technical expert who made them.

The big question for organisations and decision-makers everywhere is: What does it take to run a profitable business while still achieving the trust of the community and a social license to operate, and what are these outcomes worth?

Moving on

How do we know we're ready to move into the exciting step of finding solutions? Quite simply, if stakeholders are confident the right people are around the table and have a shared understanding of the dilemma and the collaborative process they will use to co-create the solution, then it's time.

Completing Steps One, Two and Three represents solid progress towards a solution. It may not feel like it, because the collaborative process so far may have been messy rather than linear and straightforward and may have required a different set of skills and internal resilience.

It may also feel slow and exhausting, with many participants wanting to jump quickly into solution mode. But when an enthusiastic and prepared team is ready and willing to collaborate to solve an agreed dilemma together, it is amazing what can be achieved.

This is our message. Where most project managers and decision-makers want to focus on finding a solution they believe everyone will recognise and support once it's discovered, we know that an early investment of energy and resources builds the type of trust, understanding and positive relationships that will shorten the project time. We also believe that a wiser and more innovative solution will be found.

When trust, mutual respect and positive relationships have been created, running a thoughtful, concentrated deliberative process becomes easy. So it's quite appropriate that this book's content intentionally focuses on the importance and particulars of these early stages where success provides the momentum for solution generation.

It becomes the snowball that starts rolling and getting bigger. In fact, if the first three steps of Collaborative Governance are done well, a fast, innovative and enduring solution almost always follows.

We believe that involving people in the process creates mutual respect. Appreciation of stakeholder value is the foundation element for Collaborative Governance. Sharing the definition of the dilemma builds on that. Involving stakeholders in designing both a process and a governance structure for working together continues the process by including all stakeholders in that important conversation.

When stakeholders see their fingerprints all over a collaborative decision-making process that they all own and believe is fair and equitable, then confidence builds.

By the end of Step Three, it's necessary for stakeholders to have full ownership of the solution-finding and decision-making processes so they can move ahead with energy and enthusiasm towards Step Four. The partners in the collaboration will have shared the process options, considered the context and the resources available and co-designed both the governance structure and broader communication process.

Key Learnings from Chapter 6

• Designing a collaborative process only makes sense once all parties are ready to make a commitment, and when the definition of the dilemma is supported.

• If people don't step into co-designing a process, chances are this is because they're not comfortable about a sponsor's commitment to collaborate or they are not confident that the prevailing dilemma has been defined to their satisfaction.

• If a governance structure is imposed on collaborators it is likely to call into question the intent and integrity of the process.

• The governance structure and engagement process is likely to differ – what is important is that it has been co-designed and is supported.

• It's beneficial not to overly complicate the design; the simpler the better.

• Co-designing is best done with a relatively small number of interested parties who have different interests – diversity is a key ingredient to designing a creative process that will be supported.

• When trust, mutual respect and positive relationships have been created, running a thoughtful, concentrated deliberative process becomes easy.

Chapter 7

Step Four – Co-creating the Solution

> *"Curiosity is one of the most permanent and certain characteristics of a vigorous mind."*
>
> Samuel Johnson

> *"Creative novelty springs largely from the rearrangement of the existing knowledge, a rearrangement that is itself an addition to knowledge."*
>
> J. Kneller

Co-create solutions by exploring options, evaluating impacts and deliberating decisions

We said at the start of Chapter Five that sometimes people love the challenge of finding solutions so much they spend time doing it even before they have an actual problem to solve. This has, all too frequently, been our experience. Engaging stakeholders in looking for a solution seems to be the place where clients typically realise they need some help. That's when they call Twyfords. As such, we've repeatedly witnessed firsthand the inherent problems associated with attempting to run solution-finding processes when there has been no commitment to collaboration by the decision-makers, no exploration of the dilemma and no agreed and clear process for finding a solution.

We've seen how hard it can be to co-create solutions in instances where the first three steps of the collaborative model have simply not been recognised as fundamental building blocks of collaboration. We've seen people almost set themselves up for failure by jumping straight from problem recognition into solution-generation. In most cases, success results from bringing people together armed with a clear understanding of the problem and with clear guidelines for what a good solution will look like. Without these clear boundaries, some stakeholders have a tendency to throw their sometimes ill-informed opinions on the table and then fight with everyone who disagrees with them. Other stakeholders, meantime, are intimidated or confused by the heated debates and lack of process.

In these instances, leaders who don't receive useful data from the engagement activities or build positive relationships with stakeholders shrug their shoulders and say, "We shouldn't have done this. We should just have worked out the best solution ourselves and saved ourselves all this time, expense and angst. This stuff just doesn't work."

With that in mind, we anticipate that a lot of people picking up this book may be responding to the promise that collaboration will provide them with wiser and more innovative solutions to their complex problems. They want to collaborate because of these promises.

However, if they are already at Step Four in a five-step process, they will have to do a lot of backtracking in order to build the necessary process trust and ownership before making any serious progress. Thankfully, it's not too late to begin.

In our experience, any organisation that decides to collaborate without allowing sufficient time for Steps One, Two and Three will make a poor investment. A good business investment is one where the risks are low and the potential benefits are high.

Investing in Collaborative Governance but not in the relationships, trust and shared understanding made possible by the first three steps will ensure that the reverse is true.

Clients who attempt a collaborative process in the belief they can fast-track through the early parts and focus on co-creating the solution only at Step Four will almost certainly minimise the possible benefits and run the risk of failing to achieve a wiser, more innovative solution or the type of positive, trustful relationships that will be essential when it comes to implementing their decision. Instead they are likely to experience friction and resistance from the very stakeholders they wanted to work with.

We recently saw an example of a NSW Council facing the ongoing problem of insufficient inner-city parking – a situation that resulted in parking congestion for commuters and frustration for shoppers and retailers. It also caused real difficulties for providers of professional services whose clients were staying away, put off by the long walk from their cars and the risk of incurring a parking ticket.

Council identified the problem as over-utilisation of existing parking spaces. Its officers consulted retailers and local businesses most affected by the problem and responded by installing parking meters - setting a standard fee that covered the entire gamut of possible parking durations. Their aim was to drive down the demand for the existing spaces. From their perspective they had collaborated effectively with stakeholders in finding the answer and were totally unprepared for the outrage and anger that resulted when the parking meters appeared on the streets and people realised the implications of the Council's decision on their daily lives.

Tellingly, Steps One, Two and Three had been missed. The complexity of the dilemma had not been explored more broadly. The collaboration had focused on only one set of stakeholders. Council's reputation took another hit and the concept of collaboration, once again, lost any credibility as a process of co-creating innovative and wise solutions.

Sadly, clients sometimes come to us because rather than wanting to invite stakeholders to step into their dilemma and help solve it, they genuinely believe they should solve the dilemma themselves first and then persuade stakeholders to agree. However, despite their belief that this constitutes a proactive approach that will promote stakeholder or community ownership of this solution, we most often see two resulting situations. One is that the community stays away because it seems clear to them that a decision has been made and won't be changed no matter what they say. The other is that stakeholders disagree violently, become outraged and drum up noisy opposition. Neither outcome adds any value. The decision is poor, trust is lost and negative relationships result.

We want to make it clear that activities and processes outlined in this chapter will only co-create wise, innovative and informed solutions if they are undertaken as part of a comprehensive Collaborative Governance process that starts with Step One. Chapters Four, Five and Six are essential reading in order to benefit from Chapter Seven.

In Chapter Three, we described our experiences at Callan Park, the state-run mental health facility in Sydney. This is a good example of the pitfalls of jumping straight to solution.

The angry and combative community meeting around the redevelopment plan for the Callan Park site was attended by over 500 people who were furiously challenging both the definition of the problem and the solution presented by authorities.

They had been invited to the meeting to contribute to the planning for the site once the mental health facility had been moved. They had no desire to discuss the future of the site. They were determined to stop the closure of the hospital and the relocation of the facility somewhere else, and they did.

Our repeated experiences indicate that the anger prevalent in these sessions is an expression of disappointment and frustration. In the case of Callan Park the stakeholders were saying, "Why can't they understand that this facility is important and shouldn't be closed?" The health administrators were saying, "Why can't they understand that mental healthcare has improved over the last 100 years and patients need a better facility for a different kind of health care? We've taken care of that and now want some advice on how best to use this wonderful harbourside site." They were out of step and didn't realise it because the existing relationship was distrustful and negative and there had been no attempt to improve it.

We believe that a client's investment in implementing Steps One, Two and Three is tiny compared to the benefits that may ultimately eventuate.

Consider for a moment the 2010 example of the Rudd-led Australian Government and its proposed resources tax. In this instance we saw no evidence of any commitment made within government to collaborate effectively with stakeholders. We don't think the government invited stakeholders into its dilemma or invested in building relationships and trust between the mining companies, the government and the community with a view to fostering a better understanding of the situational complexities. We don't think there was good communication with the Australian taxpayer. We don't believe enough effort was made to convey information about who actually owns the minerals that are mined, the type of profits mining companies make, the risks they take to achieve them, and the need for additional revenue to provide services to other Australians. We don't believe the government invested in this kind of relationship-building and information-sharing. We don't believe the community understood what the dilemma was. It was an either/or dispute. Either the mining companies' propaganda was believed and people saw the tax as unfair, or the government's position was supported. This then created a public relations disaster for the Prime Minister.

The value for the Rudd Government of an enduring solution as a result of a fair, transparent and thoughtful collaborative process would have been huge. The financial investment required to work with a broad range of stakeholders to help them share information and learn about the different perspectives on the dilemma would have been a small fraction of that value. Such an investment might have helped all stakeholders to appreciate the complexity of the situation so that together they could have found an innovative solution that would have nullified the precursors for confrontation and hostility.

Despite the benefits that the early work will deliver, we still hear prospective clients say, "I think we can start at Step Four. While I like the model, I don't think I need steps One, Two, or Three". In these cases we wonder whether leaders are fearful that opening up an issue for debate will trigger a tsunami of uninformed opinions and result in a loss of control. We wonder whether leaders believe that solutions don't benefit from input from unqualified people. We wonder whether they are unable to appreciate that problems can look different when viewed from other perspectives. Sometimes, the problem is so clear to leaders that they can't begin to fathom that others have different views. In other words, their mindset is, "This is the problem, therefore this is the solution".

Collaboration follows from a mindset that values the input of people with passion and knowledge about the issues. Robust co-creation activities require trust between the collaborators before they can produce valuable ideas. Innovation comes from diversity and quality relationships between unlikely people.

Collaboration Draws Out New Solutions

Recently we were speaking to a senior manager who felt that collaboration sometimes tends to dumb down the solution. He has been convinced by his life experience that consensus means reducing any solution to the lowest common denominator in order to get people to agree. He contended that the best solutions arose when experts were able to bring all their knowledge to bear on a problem.

It is an interesting perspective and one that we might agree with for Cynefin's Simple or Complicated problems described in Chapter One. According to this model, the known facts in these problems will result in the same solution today and tomorrow as they did yesterday, so experts who have the known facts may well be the best people to solve the problem.

Solving such problems may have been the experience of this and other leaders. However, we simply don't believe that experts, no matter how many or how skilled, are the best people to solve problems that are complex and multi-layered.

We don't believe they are the best people to solve problems that have interrelated and interdependent causes and by their very nature resist silver bullet solutions. Potential solutions may be mutually exclusive and require trade-offs and compromises from stakeholders. Experts alone cannot provide solutions that will stick and endure without unintended consequences.

The story of a footpath built in a country town in response to an increasing demand for improved pedestrian access for its ageing citizens is a great example of what can happen when experts are left to arrive at a solution by themselves. In this instance, the local council responded by building a footpath to enable elderly residents to negotiate a difficult road crossing. Unfortunately they put the footpath on the side of the street populated by trees that seasonally dropped fruit making the footpath slippery and dangerous at the end of every summer. Pedestrian falls increased every season. While some decision-makers are concerned that engaging people will result in impractical solutions, here was an example of an impractical solution that resulted from not seeking wider community input.

In dramatic contrast, we've seen many examples of collective intelligence in action. We've seen that dialogue and deliberation can create smart solutions that no expert had thought of.

A working group involved in the creation of a wastewater management scheme in a NSW country town two decades ago was one such collective that experienced a classic "aha" moment. This extensive project entailed solving the problem created by the large number of south coast holiday homes that lacked sewage treatment options.

Compounding the issue was the fact that people who had originally bought these holiday homes as weekenders were increasingly using them as permanent residences following retirement. Delivering sewage treatment was not a problem per se, but managing the wastewater produced posed a definite challenge. An excess of good quality, treated water was fine, even advantageous, during dry times (especially considering the vast expanses of dairy farming land that occupied the region), but periods of excessive rainfall clearly posed a problem.

Then one day, during a session attended by dairy farmers and river users, somebody remembered an existing pipe that, prior to the construction of new sewage treatment plants, had released excess wastewater into the ocean in times of wet weather rather than into an already swollen river system. It quickly transpired that tapping into this wastewater release system would solve many problems. We remember the looks on the faces of the engineers as they each tried to think of a reason why it wouldn't work. None of them could. The solution was obvious to a local resident. It was obscured for those who were not aware of the existence of this outlet. It was the fact that all the right people were in the room exploring the problem together and listening to each other, which allowed them to co-create a workable result.

A similar example occurred in relation to a plan to construct a bypass around a NSW town. In this case, the project necessitated a river crossing, and it was this component that was causing a significant degree of angst. There were several possible options, yet all appeared to have major drawbacks. Then during one public meeting and information session, a farmer went over to the map and said, "Why don't you go this way?" The engineer responded that they had looked at that option and dismissed it because of swampland. The farmer looked at the engineer and said, "That's history, the swamp was drained years ago. Come with me and have a look. I am sure that would be a better route than any of these." It turns out he was right and a route was found.

While neither of these examples specifically used a collaborative process, they demonstrate that the right people with a positive relationship with the engineers and other experts in the right place with the right information allow the right conversations to take place.

This perhaps sums up Step Four. If you've actually done the early work and got the right people in the room, finding that seemingly elusive solution can be easier than you think.

It's Really All About Trust

A strong degree of trust is needed during Step Four's co-creation activities. Indeed, any lack of trust between players can lead to caution, anxiety or even fear, all of which retard creativity. For people to be genuinely creative and exhibit a willingness to try things, they have to feel sure that they're not going to be exploited or that their ideas are not going to be hijacked for somebody else's gain.

Collaborators also have to trust that what they're doing is going to deliver an outcome; that it's going to make a real difference to the sponsor in the collaboration as well as those who are currently impacted by the dilemma. If not, they're going to lose energy rapidly. They're going to say, "If nothing is going to change, what's the point of putting in time, effort, and hard work?" They've got to see Step Five in their minds in order to keep working. But they also have to have confidence that their creativity will be respected and utilised. These are the ingredients that are essential for the ultimate co-creation of a solution.

As part of its research program, Portland State University Policy Consensus Centre has found that success in co-creating solutions isn't achieved until all the varying perspectives have been accurately understood. When stakeholders talk about consensus or agreement, they're not referring to agreement in the sense that everyone is enthusiastic about the outcome.

Rather, consensus means that all points of view have been shared and understood and that the outcome is supported, not because it is everyone's preferred solution, but because it was arrived at openly and fairly and is the best solution for the group.

Our experience is the same. The opportunity to achieve a solution comes when trust is built. Trust is built through shared experiences and shared understanding and appreciation of different interests and perspectives. If collaborators believe that their needs and passions have been listened to and taken into account in decision-making, it can be easier for them to commit to a solution that doesn't necessarily reflect their original position.

The biggest breakthroughs happen when collaborators have spent enough quality time in conversation and processed all points of view. Collaborators can't be at their most creative while others are still demanding to be heard. Holding the energy and the tension until the ideas start to flow is a skill required by a collaborative facilitator.

What Does Co-Creation Look and Feel Like?

Undoubtedly, a key question is: when is a group ready to start co-creating enduring solutions? The time is likely to be right when the dilemma is clear and stakeholders are ready to move forward in an agreed process together. If the first three steps have fostered interest in the dilemma, respect for other stakeholders and a readiness to move forward together, then it's likely that the collaborators are ready to be creative. People are ready when they feel comfortable with themselves and each other. Until this point is reached, people will keep jockeying and jostling and demonstrating a lack of willingness. People are rarely prepared to give a commitment to work together if they don't think the other players are similarly committed.

When Step Four commences, stakeholders willingly step into the process co-designed in Step Three. The relationships that have developed (the ones on which the process is built) encourage new ideas to emerge. A roomful of people engaged in paired appreciative interviews can sound like the parrot house in the zoo, yet the ideas flow. Brainstorming is exciting as ideas build one upon another.

It is important to recognise that the kind of activities used in Step Four will depend on the size and complexity of the dilemma and the time available to explore and decide on solutions. The activities for community collaboration in a small town will be different from a national collaboration such as the Land and Water Forum.

However, whatever the activities that have been included in the process design, they are likely to include both small and large groups working together to generate ideas. At one end of the scale, we've been involved in situations where a small group explored a single option that was then trialed and evaluated. Then there's something like the Land and Water Forum in New Zealand, which spent 18 months meeting regularly, listening to ideas, deliberating and finally sorting through all the material and agreeing on 53 separate recommendations. The Sydney Airport Citizens' Jury came together for a weekend and then spent the following month co-writing a report. Wellington Council's Community Panel met half-a-dozen times over a few months. Hornsby Council's deliberative community forum lasted a single day.

Sometimes the process of generating ideas and coming up with a range of options to be evaluated against the criteria will be quite structured. Other times it will be free-flowing and organic. Sometimes all the collaborating stakeholders will be involved in every activity; other times small groups of collaborators will take aspects of the dilemma and come up with their own activities to find solutions.

How Can Creative Thinking Be Encouraged and Supported?
It seems a bit of a cop out to keep saying that contexts and stakeholders will determine the best way to collaborate, but it is always true. What works in one situation may not work in another despite apparent similarities.

As we have said in other parts of this book, our fundamental belief is that people, given the opportunity to think together, are naturally creative. One of Twyfords' company values is that we believe in people and their ability to create enduring solutions together. We know those are big statements and we accept that not all people in all situations will bring the same level of enthusiasm and creativity into solving every problem. However, it is always useful to get the optimists, the disinterested and the pessimists in the room together. We had one experience where, during the introductory phase of a particular collaboration, we asked everyone in the room who they were and why they had agreed to be involved. One woman said, "I'm the complainer. I'm the one who always complains about Council." Another admitted to being attracted by the free shopping vouchers promised to all who attended, while another one of our randomly-selected participants was a part-time barrister. Each had something to offer to our process.

Other Twyfords' values include:

• initiating conversations that build connections

• encouraging learning and deliberation, and

• supporting positive change.

There are many, many theories about thinking and creativity and all have their uses. Many have been produced by psychologists, others by philosophers, others by thinkers, others by professional facilitators. The kind of problem at the core of the collaboration may be illuminated by any or all of them. We have often found Edward De Bono's Six Hat thinking to be a useful framework at certain times. For those who haven't come across de Bono before, here's a quick summary of the six kinds of thinking he believes are needed in problem-solving activities:

- Process thinking (Blue Hat), thinking about the kind of thinking needed for particular situations;
- Factual thinking (White Hat), thinking about information and data and how to get it;
- Creative thinking (Green Hat), thinking about ideas, alternatives and possibilities;
- Feelings thinking (Red Hat), using intuition, hunches and gut instinct without reasons;
- Benefits thinking (Yellow Hat), finding benefits, logical support for ideas, ways ideas are useful;
- Cautions thinking (Black Hat), looking for difficulties, weaknesses or dangers, spotting risks.

We all use these thinking models to a greater or lesser degree, but some of us are more likely to have found particular kinds more useful than others. In our example above, perhaps the complaining woman would wear De Bono's Black Hat more often, which means she would be looking for difficulties, weaknesses or dangers and risks. The reward-seeking woman was perhaps more neutral and more likely to wear De Bono's White Hat, with much of her time spent thinking about information and data and how to get it. The barrister, because of his training, could find De Bono's Blue Hat useful to help him think about the kind of thinking needed for particular situations.

Some of the collaborators will be better at certain kinds of thinking than others. Good facilitators may ask groups to put on certain hats to encourage them to think creatively, to look for benefits, or to assess the risks.

To complete our story, we remember that the part-time barrister turned out to have significant local government law experience. And while he could have been seen as a potential challenge to authority, the Council's General Manager accepted him as a marvellous resource. We also found that the lady who complained was definitely a great asset - a veritable 'canary in the coalmine' doing an excellent job of keeping us all honest. Even the Shopping Voucher Lady played a valued role, sometimes asking the hard questions and demanding more information so she could better understand the context. Together we found a solution with everyone having a useful role.

Dr Kahneman's System One and Two thinking described in Chapter One is another way to understand cognitive process. Activities such as brainstorming will draw on System One's autopilot where individuals generate quick, intuitive ideas to a question. Such activities are exciting. A group of people who know each other, who have been working together for some time and who are sensitive to each other's strengths and limitations, find brainstorming energising. A question, focused clearly on one aspect of the dilemma and designed to move the group forward, elicits a flurry of ideas as people disclose their early thinking freely. All ideas are documented without judgement. The ideas are sorted, again without judgement, and another round of brainstorming looks for ways to combine those ideas creatively. A third round of brainstorming seeks new ideas that build on any of the first ideas or combinations of ideas. At the end of the brainstorming, after prioritising which ideas are worth exploring further, small groups are put to work to examine what further information is required to allow a particular idea to be better understood. This includes examining its potential benefits as well as its difficulties, weaknesses, dangers and inherent risks.

As we have noted before, ideas generated by System One thinking are often seriously affected by subconscious intuition and biases. This is why such ideas need to be expanded and explored using a System Two approach, where different, more thoughtful ideas can be generated by groups systematically working through known facts and perspectives while creatively exploring possibilities.

We have also been influenced in our work by a wonderful book edited by Sam Kaner called *A Facilitator's Guide to Participatory Decision Making*. Sam and his fellow authors Lenny Lind, Catherine Toldi, Sarah Fisk and Duane Berger have created a practical book full of tools designed to help increase participation and collaboration in group thinking so that effective, inclusive and participatory decisions can be made.

Kaner and his colleagues make a useful distinction between divergent thinking and convergent thinking and the need for both in thoughtful group processes. Divergent thinking refers to a deviation from the everyday thinking processes we employ for our regular day-to-day activities. In Edward de Bono's Six Hat Thinking, this might mean putting on the Green Hat for creativity, which involves coming up with ideas, alternatives and possibilities.

It might mean putting on the Red Hat for feelings, which involves using intuition, hunches and gut instinct. It will probably mean using both. Divergent thinking is exciting, energising work, particularly for groups ready for Step Four, who trust each other and recognise that by working together, the ideas will get better and better.

However, divergent thinking may also involve listening to other perspectives, listening to people you may not agree with, listening to people you may dislike, listening to what seem like dumb ideas. Not everyone finds it easy. Divergent thinking requires the use of both our advocacy and inquiry skills; being able to articulate clearly our own thinking and ideas while persuading others to our point of view. It also requires us to be able to listen, question and explore the potential of others' ideas while also being open to persuasion.

Things can get messy as collaborators try to get their heads around what the ideas mean and the potential they offer for the future. This is the phase we refer to as The Groan Zone - the time when all the ideas are buzzing around and everyone is challenged to process and understand them while making sense out of the implications they have for solving the dilemma.

It can be a difficult zone to work in. It can take time and patience requiring a different set of skills from all players. But people will step into this if they trust the process they are using and will, eventually, become ready to move into a period of convergent thinking.

This is when the involvement of too many collaborators can become a challenge. Indeed, it takes high quality facilitation to support a large group through intense, concentrated and sometimes emotional sessions and keep them focused. Calling for breaks will be necessary to keep the energy going.

Convergent thinking uses the skills of combining, building, prioritising, grouping, culling and summarising. During convergent thinking the collaborators leave behind the ordinary and start working only with the ideas that fly. It can be a tough time, too, because it requires testing ideas for their potential to solve the problem and discarding those that don't make the cut.

People wearing Green Hats try to combine ideas in unusual ways. People wearing Red Hats explore their gut reaction to ideas. People with Black and Yellow Hats systematically work through the impacts of each idea. Yellow Hats look for positives. Black Hats look for risks and possible problems.

The Institute of Cultural Affairs (ICA) is another group (helpful for Step

Four activities) offering creative ways to encourage collaboration. They have developed a suite of methods to help groups think, talk and work together. Information about their Technology of Participation, or ToP, can be found at http://topfacilitation.net/. The activities described as part of ToP include ways to encourage community groups to find solutions to their own problems which focus on content, concerns, issues and ideas. Their techniques encourage groups to think experientially and draw on both emotion and logic in their search for innovative and creative solutions.

People learn in different ways and it's important to provide opportunities for all stakeholders in the room to work at their best. Visual learners will benefit from working with pictures, diagrams and other visual representations, and will enjoy opportunities to draw their ideas and thoughts rather than writing them down. Others will need to work kinesthetically, using materials and their hands to explore ways of solving problems. Others will be quite comfortable using words to describe their ideas and thoughts.

The Power of Deliberation
Whatever processes or tools are used to encourage convergent thinking, it is certain that the wisest and most creative solutions will emerge from quality deliberation. Deliberation is the weighing up of alternatives, the thoughtful consideration of pros and cons. It is about asking questions, using inquiry, questioning and investigating. This represents a far different approach from advocacy, which involves stating, arguing for, and defending one's position. Dialogue, not debate, is a key to effective deliberation.

Deliberation can be fostered in many ways. Typically, it involves a group of people who in some way represent a broader community of interest. They are provided with the opportunity to learn about an issue in some depth, to think about it, talk it over, perhaps weigh up the pros and cons and ultimately come to a position. An example of a deliberative process is a Citizens' Jury, where randomly selected community members come together to deliberate on a complex issue. This model takes its lead from the legal system where randomly selected juries deliberate and decide the fate of those accused of serious crime. Citizens' Juries are used very successfully to provide advice to decision-makers on preferred solutions to very complex community dilemmas.

Other deliberative processes include deliberative forums, consensus conferences, and even on-line forums. In each case, participants are encouraged and empowered to learn, think, talk together, and ultimately arrive at a thoughtful position.

One of the leading thinkers in the field of deliberation and consensus-building is Lawrence Susskind, who has developed the Mutual Gains Approach to solution-finding. Susskind writes about the power of inviting people together to find a solution that is more creative, more enduring and 'better' than what any group could have come up with on its own. The Mutual Gains Approach tells us that diverse groups can find solutions that effectively create value, which Susskind likens to "making the pie bigger". To this end Susskind has developed a rigorous process for working with diverse groups on controversial projects to achieve solutions that do create additional value.

One of the keys to a successful consensus-building process, according to Susskind, is the right convenor. For Susskind, the Convenor is a critical role that brings the parties together and usually finances the process. In simple situations, identifying the convener is often straightforward. For more complex dilemmas, Susskind tells us that identifying the appropriate Convenor can be a challenge in itself.

We have also found the role of the Convenor to be particularly valuable. When trust is low and a community has a poor relationship with an organisation, an independent, respected convenor plays an important role in bringing the parties together to talk. The Convenor or sponsor understands the importance of process and the need for people to think, learn and talk together. By their independence the Convenor creates a space in which a deliberative process can take place and from which enduring solutions can emerge. For these reasons, an important question when working with people to co-create solutions is: who is going to convene this discussion and how?

One final thought relates to the benefits we have found when using the Appreciative Inquiry method in our group work. Indeed, the model of discover, dream, design and destiny has proven very helpful.

Building on what we want more of, imagining what a situation could be at its best, then defining those provocative propositions and creating the pathway to success is a powerful tool for triggering group creativity.

The Appreciative Inquiry model supports collaborative governance in many aspects. It's about achieving positive change by focusing on what things could be like if optimum potential was achieved. It's about exploring what has worked in the past, analysing the factors which supported that success, and assessing how such factors can be replicated in the future. Using appreciative interviews to understand what the situation looks like now when it is at its best, dreaming about what it could look like if all the existing strengths and opportunities were explored, then working together to design what could be, is essentially what Collaborative Governance is about.

The final step in Appreciative Inquiry is about the destiny of the change and how to make it happen. This is the subject of our next chapter on co-delivery of actions.

The individual strengths and preferences within the group will be well known by the time Step Four is reached, so selecting the most effective ways of encouraging their creativity will be easier. Whatever the activities designed to support creativity, the objective is to allow every individual within the collaborative process to learn in the way most appropriate to them, to contribute in the way most appropriate to them and to support others in the group to do the same.

The output of this part of Step Four could be one preferred solution that the group already agrees on. It could be a shortlist of options that need a more structured assessment against the decision criteria generated in Step Two. It could be a series of possibilities that may require balances or trade-offs in their implementation, thus necessitating more information and assistance from specific stakeholders.

Be aware that there may be times where some stakeholders are ready to move to a decision while others are not. This can create a delicately poised environment that may even give rise to a bout of campaign rush by those who claim to be ready. Rather than acknowledging that people may be at different stages, a prevailing attitude among some may be, "We're ready, why aren't you?" Some will sift through and assess ideas quickly and others will take longer. To be effective the process can't be hurried, despite demands, expectations, or pressures to do so. If some people are stuck, it's vital that all the players in the room maintain a creative and collaborative space. If any of the players lose focus and stop trying, this can have a ripple effect through the process. Everybody in the room has a role in ensuring that the lines of communication remain open. Be patient. Success is close at hand.

The Ultimate Test
So, you've negotiated Step Four with collaborators who have used the knowledge and the robust relationships they developed through Steps One, Two and Three, been well-facilitated through many Step Four group activities and have generated and refined the resulting ideas into a list of agreed options. Now it's necessary to spend time evaluating the potential impacts of each of the surviving options. White Hat, Red Hat, Yellow Hat and Black Hat thinking is required here. Systematic System Two thinking is required as well. This means more hard but necessary work to make sure the impacts of each option have been rigorously assessed from everyone's point of view. Who will this option affect, and in what way? Is the option likely to cause unintended consequences for any stakeholder? Will it impact on any stakeholders who are not part of the collaboration?

It may be that some of the stakeholders, who until this point haven't been active in the collaborative process, need to be invited in to consider the potential impacts of options on them in the short, medium and longer-term. Remember, one of the aims of the collaboration is that the agreed solution or solutions should be acceptable to all stakeholders. The communications strategy put in place during Step Three needs to provide opportunities for any stakeholders likely to be affected by a new potential solution to be given a chance to assess impacts to avoid unintended consequences.

Finally, once the options have been fully explored, the collaborators may find a deliberative process useful so that all the relevant information on the potential solutions and their impacts can be made available, and so that the necessary time and space can be allocated for consensus to be reached.

For the group to reach consensus, each collaborator must believe that a solution or combination of solutions appropriately addresses the dilemma. The deliberative process is structured so that the previously defined decision-making criteria developed in Step Two is used to test the options. The criteria that the collaborators developed after asking themselves what mattered to them about the solution now become the parameters by which they consider, reflect and deliberate. This activity will give everyone confidence that they've nailed a solution.

Bear in mind that the criteria developed may not each carry the same weight. For example, a bridge or a stadium needs to stay up and not fall down under certain pressures, so being structurally sound and appropriately engineered are design criteria that must carry the greatest importance. Aesthetics may well be an important factor but they can't be pursued at the expense of structural integrity. Or can they? Let's say the stadium roof is going to be joined to an iconic building such as the Leaning Tower of Pisa, or that the bridge is going to be constructed over a culturally sensitive historic site. Maybe now the aesthetics are just as important as the structure's strength.

While such decisions must include all perspectives, applying technical criteria will in general be easier than applying value-based criteria and certainly easier for many collaborators to agree on.

Distinguishing the essential from the desirable criteria and then placing them in order of importance will be one conversation collaborators can expect to have. At the end of the day, if this stage is done well, no one will know where the solution really came from. It will have been the creation of the group. No one individual will be able to claim victory because the solution will have emerged organically from the conversations, relationships, and collective knowledge of the group. Because of the foundations that have been laid, trust between players will be palpable. All vested interests will have long evaporated. Perhaps this is hard to believe until it has been experienced, but we believe it because we experience it regularly in our work.

By the end of Step Four, it's necessary for stakeholders to have participated fully in the co-creation process and agreed on a solution to the dilemma before progressing to Step Five. The partners in the collaboration will have explored the options, evaluated the impacts of each option from each stakeholder perspective and agreed on the solution after participating in a deliberation.

Key Learnings from Chapter 7

- If collaborators believe that their needs and passions have been listened to and taken into account in decision-making, it can be easier for them to commit to a solution that doesn't necessarily reflect their original position.

- Given the opportunity to think together, people are naturally creative, and more so when they believe they are respected and their interests are understood.

- Processes for divergent and convergent thinking are both needed to help a group generate consensus to a creative solution.

- Appreciative inquiry and deliberative processes make for a powerful combination when stakeholders are truly ready to find a way forward.

- Revisiting the criteria established when defining the dilemma is a crucial step in deciding whether the solution is going to endure.

Chapter 8

Step Five – Co-Delivering Actions

> *"The improvement of understanding is for two ends:*
> *first, our own increase of knowledge;*
> *secondly, to enable us to deliver that knowledge to others."*
>
> John Locke

Co-deliver actions by determining governance structure for implementation, agreeing stakeholder roles and responsibilities and establishing a monitoring and evaluation framework.

This final step takes us to the end of decision-making and into the new space of implementation. It's the end we had in mind from the beginning. It's the time when the collaboration fulfils the meaning of "enduring" in relation to the designated solution. It's the time stakeholders and the sponsoring organisation act to achieve the desired outcomes so that the solution is implemented successfully, thus avoiding the unintended consequences that so often follow change processes.

Clearly, the solution co-created through Steps One to Four only endures if it is implemented successfully. This requires action and effort, and who better to provide much of that action and effort than those whose energy, enthusiasm and persistence co-created the solution in the first place?

Luckily, the energy, knowledge and trust needed to provide this necessary action and effort has been built up during the preceding steps. During this final step of Co-delivery, it's important to know how to draw on and utilise the social capital, readiness, energy and excitement that has been generated within the process.

We've talked a lot about the establishment of mutual trust as one of the key foundations of collaborative governance. This mutuality is important.

Collaborators trust the sponsoring organisation to ensure their work will contribute to real change. When stakeholders are confident that the outcome of their collaborative process will influence the sponsoring organisation's decisions, they are much more likely to collaborate willingly and with energy.

In the same way, the sponsoring organisation trusts its fellow collaborators to be genuine in their attempts to find a solution that works for everyone, including the sponsor. When the sponsoring organisation really trusts their fellow collaborators and the process in which they have all invested to co-create an innovative solution to a problem they all share, the process is much more likely to have the positive outcomes they all desire.

There is a promise inherent in the collaborative governance process that, once a solution is found, the sponsoring organisation will implement it. The International Association for Public Participation (IAP2) suggests that the sponsoring organisation's promise to collaborating stakeholders should be: "We will look to you for direct advice and innovation in formulating solutions and incorporate your advice and recommendations into decisions to the maximum extent possible." The collaborators have a right to expect the implementation process to start as quickly as possible after they have done their work and recommended solutions to the dilemma.

In the same way, the sponsoring organisation can also expect the stakeholders to assume a role in the implementation. The most effective way to harness the energy and enthusiasm of those stakeholders is to ask them how best they can be part of the change. The sponsoring organisation may well ask them what kind of decision-making or governance structure may be appropriate for the implementation phase. They may ask them what kind of role the collaborators could or would like to play, and what resources they would need to fulfill that role.

Collaborators who have themselves committed to the process, worked on achieving the required clarity together, understood and developed the collaborative process and structure for decision-making and created the solutions, will be in an excellent position to address any difficulties or roadblocks sometimes associated with implementation. These stakeholders have had plenty of practice at collaboration and often want to share some of the responsibility for implementation rather than watch others who might not understand all the commitment, dedication, negotiation and deliberation that went on throughout the collaborative process. In fact, it's our experience that if encouraged and appropriately used, the energy and enthusiasm created by the first four steps will continue.

As part of working together to progress the delivery of the solution, the leaders within the sponsoring organisation will need to demonstrate how they will resource the necessary implementation and make the solution happen.

It's also a good idea for the sponsoring organisation to publicly acknowledge and celebrate the success of the collaboration, the hard work of the collaborators and the wisdom of the solution to be implemented, as the first activity in Step Five.

An early action is creating a strategy for promoting both the process and the outcome to those who weren't part of it and who may question the wisdom of the solution. After the Land and Water Forum handed its recommendations to the relevant New Zealand Ministers in 2010, the Chair, Alastair Bisley, and a group of collaborating stakeholders were asked to visit other stakeholders around the country to explain the Forum process and its recommendations.

Another technique that may be used to share the learning of process and outcome with those who were not part of the journey is action learning. Action Learning is a process for drawing learning from experience. At its simplest, it consists of two stages: action and reflection. These can then be built into the Collaborative Governance cycles. The reflection gains its point by leading to learning.

By applying action learning at each stage of the Collaborative Governance process, we expand the reflection component and take into account that it is partly a critical review of the last action and also, partly, a plan for what will happen next. If we add "theory" or principles to this, we start to make sense of the world in ways that build on our prior understanding. In enhancing that understanding, we become better able to act in the future.

When we are acting, we often don't have the time to be deliberate about what we are doing (System One thinking). The "theories" we draw on are intuitive theories. In review and planning, our theories can be made explicit (System Two thinking). In other words, action is informed by intuitive theories (System One). Critical review and planning are informed by conscious theories and assumptions (System Two). These theories are derived deliberately from recent experience and used to plan the next experience. You could say, then, that action learning functions by a dual alternation: between action and reflection; between unconscious and conscious theories. By engaging with both of these in a cyclic procedure, we enable all stakeholders to learn and contribute to how best to implement the next step.

While many of the stakeholders will want to step into the actions involved in solution co-deliverance, it's important to recognise that not all of them will have the time or resources to continue after successfully co-creating the solution. However, it's our experience that most will want some input into Step Five. It is important not to expect too much and to allow each collaborating stakeholder to indicate the roles and responsibilities they can take on, with appropriate resourcing.

Some Stories of Stakeholder Commitment
We have experienced some really inspiring times when stakeholders (in their enthusiasm for the collaborative work they've done) have not only stayed with the project, but added to it in ways that have exceeded everyone's expectations.

One of these occasions occurred when we ran a collaborative visioning process in a NSW country town. Those who attended were quite excited about being asked to participate and were able to contribute significantly to the community vision. However, some expressed concern that not all of their fellow citizens had been given the same opportunity. We explained that sadly this was unavoidable due to limited time and budgetary constraint, but that a broader communication strategy was in place to share the information. Without even asking us, the group subsequently decided to organise an activity on their own. They invited people interested but unable to attend the initial session and designed a process during which they modeled the collaborative process, sharing the dilemma and the work that had been done in the collaborative session. We were surprised when they brought the results of their community meeting back to us with stories of the responses. Tellingly, they had taken the initiative as a result of their own positive experience of being asked, acknowledged, and listened to. The energy that was created in the first process lived on.

The importance and potential of collaborative energy has been noted by many. In his book *The Wisdom of Crowds* (mentioned previously in Chapter Four), James Surowiecki writes about the huge amounts of people who instinctively collaborate as they use the busy sidewalks of New York. He observes that everybody is part of the solution, that everybody makes minor adjustments when walking on these narrow sidewalks to make it possible for each person to get where they want to go. It's got nothing to do with anyone telling people what to do or how to do it. It just kind of happens of its own accord because everyone knows that they're in it together.

Similar collaborative energy and instinct is evident among herd animals and birds. In order to survive deadly Antarctic winter temperatures, Emperor penguins huddle together in a way that acts as a windbreak. All the penguins move, constantly shuffling from inside to outside the group to ensure that each of them takes their turn at being exposed to the wind before retreating into the warmth of the collective. They all move independently but they all move as part of a whole.

Both are analogies for what happens when an action as part of implementing a solution is truly co-delivered. Just like the New York natives and the Emperor penguins, stakeholders 'co-delivering actions to implement a solution they understand, co-operate because they have recognised the wisdom of the solution and want it to work.

Room For Everyone

Co-operation in action doesn't have to come only from those who are committed and enthusiastic. Anything but an exclusive club, anyone and everyone can be a part of an energetic process. Consider the following four stories that illustrate different ways that collaborators and others have stepped forward to take part in solution implementation:

Story One:

During the worst of Sydney's recent drought, a decision was made to make some significant changes to the workings of Warragamba Dam so that water at the base of the dam (previously inaccessible to water users), could be pumped into the system via the installation of a new pump station. The construction work was undertaken over a period of some six months and had a significant impact on those living in the small town of Warragamba. Some collaboration was undertaken between those responsible for the construction and the local residents. Many residents were very concerned about the dangers of heavy truck movements in the town and a range of safety issues was considered. As a result, plans were put in place to minimise the risks. During this process, one resident asked, "Why would you put trucks through the town where there's a school and a child care centre? When all the kids come out it will be hazardous to their safety." This person, because of his genuine concern, adopted a role as monitor of all truck movements. He wanted to make sure the truckies kept to the strict timeframes and routes set down in the plans. He logged times and dates of infringements, he documented the registration numbers of the offending trucks and even noted physical descriptions of the drivers responsible. As a result, there wasn't a truck driver working on the project that didn't drive more carefully, knowing they were likely to be reported for any transgression. In the end, this person had a direct input into the implementation of the solution. His contribution was valuable to both the construction and the town.

Story Two:

This one relates to the time we designed and facilitated a citizens' panel whose job was to learn about, deliberate on and provide recommendations to a council's Long-Term Council Community Plan. In all, the panel met five times, the process culminating in a report with recommendations for council. Once the panel had worked through its recommendations, it was time to write a report. We were keen for this report to be written by a small volunteer group of panellists so that it would be seen, both by councillors and other panellists, as "their" report, as well as "their" recommendations. However, we were unsure as to whether such a task would be willingly taken on, as writing a report had not been part of the original agreement. So we were delighted when six volunteers put up their hands after the hard work of agreeing on the recommendations had been completed. They believed in the process they'd been involved with and wanted to ensure that their report honoured and acknowledged the work of the panel.

Story Three:

We once worked with a Sydney council who wanted its community to help with the design of a new Aquatic Centre. A deliberative process had been established to make some decisions about what the essential inclusions needed to be. Council was replacing an old, unsafe pool and it was important that the cost of the new centre fell within its defined infrastructure budget. It was also important that the new facility contained features that would ensure its use by all demographics. Once initial recommendations had been co-created by the group, it became evident that some additional decisions still needed to be made once some additional information was obtained. In response to this need, those who'd been involved over the previous couple of weekends got together and organised another meeting on their own. They then provided an additional report, which council subsequently incorporated into their decision-making process. The original deliberative process generated a great deal of enthusiasm among those involved. The stakeholders' collective response seemed to be, "You've asked us to be involved and it's important. While we haven't agreed on everything so far, we're still willing to work".

Story Four:

Our most powerful example of collaborative energy potential occurred around the work we did at Sydney Airport. One recruit for that particular citizens' jury was a woman named Jill from Zimbabwe. On the first day, she made a point of saying that the opportunity to make a contribution to a project of this nature as a new Australian citizen was an incredible honour. As fate would have it, the next day she had a car accident on her way to the jury session. Thankfully not seriously injured, she rang to apologise and say she might be a bit late. Sydney Airport Corporation told her not to worry, as they would pay her anyway. But she clung to the importance of being involved. When she turned up later that day she was on crutches and had lacerations on her face. Despite her injuries she stayed with the whole process. Several days later, Jill ended up in hospital with a blood clot in her leg. Again, she called and apologised, wanting to stay with the process. The group was putting their report together so documents were faxed to the hospital so that she could make comments from her bed. She was absolutely unstoppable and doggedly determined to play her part.

When people are considered, acknowledged, recognised and valued, the resulting enthusiasm is amazing and can take everybody a bit by surprise.

Organisations, associations and businesses often struggle with the question of where necessary resources are going to come from, but from stories like these we can plainly see that their own stakeholders represent perhaps the greatest untapped resource of all. Such collaborative processes can create a range of benefits for those who participate, including improved knowledge and understanding of how difficult it can be to satisfy the disparate needs and expectations of stakeholders, and how important it is to find informed and implementable solutions that are at least acceptable to the majority.

While coming up with a decision or a solution is one thing, we can see that the privilege of being involved and the responsibility participation entails builds and perpetuates something more far-reaching and powerful.

Such inspiring anecdotes bring to mind a wonderful quote by Elizabeth Moss Kanter: *"Change is disturbing when it's done to us, it's exhilarating when it's done by us."* Once this exhilaration gains momentum, it's surprising what can actually be created.

The 2000 Sydney Olympics not only demonstrated how collective energy can be harnessed, but also how it can become infectious. The bid team had laid the groundwork so that when Sydney was announced as the Olympic city, it wasn't just the Premier who leapt to his feet and cheered. A large proportion of Sydney-siders leapt and cheered with him. They took ownership of their Olympic Games. The call for volunteers was oversubscribed, with people of all ages stepping forward from all walks of life.

The Olympic spirit was lived and breathed by volunteers, local residents and ticket holders on a mass scale. Everybody contributed, even down to parking in the right places and catching the right trains and buses. People were happily corralled onto public transport. Ticket holders willingly queued in the pre-determined manner. Residents proactively played their part when an event was held in their suburb. Everyone smiled and the positive energy and spirit of mass collaboration was indomitable.

What It Takes to Co-Deliver Actions

The collaborative governance model suggests that all internal and external stakeholders – the sponsoring organisation, its leaders and project managers and the groups with whom they collaborated - need to do four things:
- consider what implementation will look like, how the recommendations for solution will be taken forward, who will take them forward and who will continue to make the decisions about their implementation;
- consider what roles, responsibilities and accountabilities stakeholders in the collaboration could assume in the implementation phase;
- create an Action Plan for implementation of the solution so that an agreed future is clear to all;
- establish a monitoring and evaluation framework for implementation.

Sometimes the governance structure for implementation will remain the same as for the collaboration, although there may well be a change in personnel within the various parts of the structure. Some people's skills are more appropriate to creating answers to problems, while others are better at getting things done.

However, it's possible that implementing the solution may require a new governance structure. This may become necessary in the event of new groups becoming involved, or the governance process becoming contained within the sponsoring organisation.

The context will, once again, determine the best way to go. The important part of co-delivering actions is that everyone understands what will happen next and knows who is responsible and accountable for making it happen. Before celebrating the success of the collaborative process and allowing all the collaborators to go back to their day jobs, it is useful for each stakeholder to be asked whether they have an interest in taking on an implementation role. However, it is dangerous to ask that question unless there is a genuine opportunity for them to take on such a role. It is frustrating to accept a role in a project or process only to be subsequently left out or ignored. It could be enough to destroy the positive relationships created by the collaborative process. So don't ask the question if the implementation action plan is already in place or doesn't offer genuine roles to collaborators.

It may be more useful for the stakeholders to be involved in establishing the monitoring and evaluation framework for the implementation and take a monitoring role, somewhat like our Warragamba resident in the story above.

This is not the right place to go into detail about how to establish a monitoring and evaluation framework for the implementation process. That's a job for the implementation team. Later in this chapter we will talk about how best to review and evaluate the collaboration process itself. However, it's our experience that collaborators will be keen to follow the progress of the implementation and to learn whether the solution they helped create has been a success.

They will have a particular perspective on the success factors that they expect to see from the solution. This will reflect the perspective they took into the collaboration, which helped them co-define the dilemma and talk about what mattered to them about the solution. They will want to see whether the positive change they sought has resulted when the solution has been implemented. So, they are likely to want to help establish the performance indicators for that success. It will be useful to ask them: What do you expect to see if the solution has been implemented effectively? This could be an exciting question for collaborators. When they define what success would look like to them, they are in a position to act as monitors. The Warragamba resident wanted to see safe truck driving so that residents weren't endangered during the construction of the pump station. He was prepared to take enormous amounts of trouble to monitor whether that happened and to let the project managers know when it didn't. He collected information that the construction managers would otherwise have had to pay observers to gather. And he did it voluntarily every day.

Collaborators can also keep watch to see whether any unintended consequences have resulted from the solution's implementation. Having discussed the risks of the solution during Step Four, they are in a position to identify them and give the implementation early warning of possible negative outcomes so appropriate actions can be taken. Never underestimate what a collaborator will be prepared to do to ensure the success of the solution they co-created.

A Life Beyond

After all the hard work to build energy, trust and appreciation, the journey shouldn't end with the delivery and implementation of a great enduring solution. Although it's very easy to believe that the job is over once a decision has been made, we believe that maintaining the legacy of the collaborative process is crucial. Indeed, co-implementation should be viewed as a great way of building capacity for the future. What we end up with, if we do this piece right, is a working framework for the future. It's about building a capacity to implement and to come back and start again when the next problem comes over the hill. When people within an organisation say, "We want to work with you on this, we've been involved before, we understand it, so let's get on with it", it's a clear indication that this capacity has been achieved. That capacity can be extremely useful when it comes to stepping into the next challenging activity.

To us, the last step of the journey is to make sure that it isn't over. The implementation of an enduring solution is an opportunity to reflect on the process and the outcomes that have been delivered. It's an opportunity to not only celebrate the windfalls, but also to make sure that the desire and willingness that made them possible doesn't disappear. It's about taking it forward, maintaining the energy, allowing people to take up responsibility and authority and do things on their own. Who knows where things might lead?

In our work with a number of organisations who have used collaborative governance, we have defined the success factors of the collaborative governance process as being:

• a mandate to address an issue or group of related issues from a recognised decision-making body which itself has serious regard for the collaboration and will not allow it to be subverted;

- appropriate resourcing with funding coming from the decision-making body; the resources the collaborative process has at its disposal should be utilised for the benefit of the process as a whole;

- stakeholders in the problem may be invited to step in to a collaborative process but will make their own decision whether or not to participate;

- stakeholders who participate in a collaboration must believe they have a real, inescapable and unconstrained responsibility to reach a consensus on a solution to the initial problem;

- participants need to be provided with information on the economic, social, cultural and environmental aspects of the problem to be solved as well as valid, reliable and relevant scientific information in order to allow the participants to come to an integrated understanding about the extent of the problem and the potential solutions;

- autonomy, independence, space and time for collaborators to do their work; confidence among collaborators that their work will contribute to real change; sufficient time but also time constraints and a realistic timetable;

- open and transparent processes that will inevitably be messy and unpredictable;

- a skilled independent facilitator or chair;

- clarity about participants' individual and shared responsibilities for achieving consensus, approving the report and planning subsequent implementation.

There is value in this final step, in spending time with all the collaborators to check their collaborative process against these success factors. Learning how to do something better next time depends on seriously assessing both what went well in the collaboration and what could have been improved.

Asking questions that explore the process used and documenting accurately and truthfully what worked and what didn't and why, will help others who follow. This means seeking volunteers to write the report. This may not be difficult. There may be willing volunteers among the collaborators to do not just that, but to also find a place for their report to be published so it becomes accessible to others who follow.

Thoughts to Ponder

Glen Lauder, one of our valued New Zealand colleagues, said recently: "Sometimes the results of deliberative processes don't have to be decisions. They might simply be people walking away and acting in concert". While we believe that collaborative governance is about collaborative decision-making, this was a really interesting perspective; that you could have a really useful collaborative process and outcomes stemming from a collective recognition that something just needs to be done; like the Emperor penguins, the sidewalk users in New York, or local communities during the Sydney Olympics.

Perhaps an involvement in deliberative processes can subsequently inspire or influence people to act for the collective good just because it feels like the right and sensible thing to do. Such an eventuality would enable a subtle and internal decision to occur within everybody.

But it won't have been the result of an overt decision-making process, but rather more of a covert agreement. Indeed, Professor Lyn Carson, an academic expert on democracy and public policy, says that our participatory muscle atrophies through lack of use, and that once we activate it, it's hard to turn off. Consequently, we find other, perhaps less productive ways, of using it.

If people have their wider capacities built through collaborative practice, it might mean that partnerships could be more easily developed and that relationships between different stakeholder groups may lead to other benefits far beyond a particular issue. Perhaps part of this last step is asking questions about what we can all do. What are the opportunities that our solution and subsequent decision has created for us? How can we learn to implement the Power of 'Co' ourselves?

What may ultimately evolve is a system of organic behaviour where every player instinctively plays a role commensurate with the common good. You can't plan it and you can't direct it, it just works.

American political scientist Robert Putnam, in his book *"Bowling Alone: The Collapse and Revival of American Community"*, makes a distinction between two kinds of social capital: bonding capital and bridging capital. Bonding occurs when people socialise with people who are like them: same age, same race, same religion, and so on. But in order to create peaceful societies in a diverse multi-ethnic country, Putnam says bridging capital is needed. Bridging capital grows when you make friends with people who are not like you, such as supporters of another football team. Putnam argues that those two kinds of social capital have historically strengthened each other. However, today people are bowling alone and not joining bowling leagues which is a sign of declining in bonding capital. This, Putnam believes, inevitably creates a decline of the bridging capital leading to the greater ethnic tensions we are seeing in society today. Putnam talks about the future of our societies that are becoming increasingly pluralistic and cosmopolitan and asks how we might actually build bridges and bridging capital between people with different sets of values who see the world differently. With this in mind, the emergence of intuitive, trusting, constructive, deliberative, sympathetic processes and mindsets (the very type nurtured by collaborative governance processes) could be a way forward into a more resilient society.

Key Learnings from Chapter 8

- A solution only endures if implemented successfully

- Those who create a solution are best placed to implement it

- Those who have collaborated with each other to creat a solution are better prepared to work together to overcome barriers to implementation

Chapter 9

A Positive Note
On Which to End

"If we all knew what we all know, just imagine the possibilities."

As we have said in the previous chapters, our collaborative governance model is a pathway that leads the user from a complex problem or dilemma to an enduring solution. The more we've explored this model, the more we've discovered the full value of its first three steps: Commit to collaboration; Co-define the dilemma; Co-design process and governance structure.

The outcomes of those three steps are essential. These are:

• an appreciation of the value of all stakeholders working together;

• strong relationships based on conversations, positive experiences and trust;

• a shared understanding of the complexity of the dilemma from all stakeholder perspectives; and

• a solution-finding process and decision-making structure that has been designed in partnership.

Without these outcomes in place, the ability to co-create solutions (by exploring options, evaluating impacts and deliberating decisions) and co-deliver actions (by determining a governance structure, stakeholder roles, responsibilities and accountabilities, and establishing a monitoring and evaluation framework) is likely to be elusive.

We recognise that many people may view our diagram as appearing a bit linear, as if the process flows in a one-way direction from Dilemma to Solution. To them, we say this: *"Collaborative Governance, as we see it, is likely to be iterative and often messy. It will involve some challenging encounters with people who think differently and who enjoy winning. It will sometimes feel directionless, sometimes frenzied and sometimes quiet and considered. It may require the slow acquisition of new lenses through which to view the world in general, including stakeholders and their perspectives."*

To our way of thinking, the co-creation of a solution first requires a smart leader to invite stakeholders to be as creative as they can. Such a leader calls on the technical expertise of brilliant people as well as those who can bring to the table different values, connections and relationships. The ultimate reward for taking this approach is the opportunity to be part of a solution that no single individual could deliver. In other words, leaders must acknowledge that expertise lies in a whole range of places. They need to encourage that expertise by providing the space and resources for creative and innovative thinking.

For Twyfords, supporting collaboration has meant establishing genuine partnerships with our clients. While they assume the business risk relating to the content (finding a solution to a problem that will drive change and produce positive and enduring outcomes), we assume the business risk relating to the process (appreciating, supporting and encouraging leaders to trust the Power of 'Co', and helping them co-define, co-design, co-create and co-deliver a solution in conjunction with their relevant stakeholders).

A real life example of the Power of 'Co'...

Eight years ago, Dale Williams, the Mayor of a small town in New Zealand's North Island, identified a strong need for youth employment opportunities. In response, he took his community along with him on a journey to find a solution. The project started with two people – himself and a local employer. Together they set a community goal of generating employment for all. They then encouraged community leaders to take ownership of the risk and negative impacts associated with high levels of disenfranchised youth. Nearly a decade on, Dale believes that achieving community ownership of the problem was the critical starting point. This enabled him to bring relevant stakeholders including employers, families, kids, schools, training institutions and community organisations into the process. Together they gathered information about employment opportunities for young people and ascertained what employers required from young employees. This took time as the community had lost its connection with some of the local employers. It was therefore important to re-establish those connections and build relationships with managers and those responsible for staffing.

In due course, relationships were re-established between employers, schools, teachers, community mentors (who connected school leavers with their future careers), training groups, young people and their families. A broad range of solutions was generated by the collaboration.

These included the better matching of training with employer needs, the availability of support for young people in their transitions between school, training and employment, and the creation of an expectation within the community that young people should work. Voluntary community initiatives such as study support, mentoring and scholarship programs were also established, as were employers' initiatives such as traineeships, work experience programs and apprenticeships. Regular celebrations of success were also a feature.

Dale knows that the community benefits resulting from full youth employment are immense. Indeed, virtually non-existent levels of crime, vandalism and graffiti are all factors that allow vulnerable and older people to feel very safe. He attributes this transformation to a change in attitude from wanting to "fix" the kids to appreciating them, wanting to help them and find ways to support them (mindset). It resulted from community understanding and ownership not only of the dilemma, but also of what mattered about the solutions (co-definition). It relied on a process of relationship-building that evolved over time as a result of working together (co-design). It involved solution-finding together (co-creation), and finally a shared delivery of the solutions that connected everyone to the outcomes (co-delivery).

Dale clearly demonstrates the Power of 'Co'. He is also clear that none of the steps in their process could have been missed, even though time was critical to their success. He acknowledges that the project continues as a work in progress. Looking back, he likens his role to that of a traffic director and general adviser. His community has taken the lead.

Why we have written this book

Our 20-plus year involvement in the field of community engagement has at times been frustrating. Often we have watched the process being driven by a compliance culture, with both public and private organisations merely engaging with stakeholders to satisfy regulatory or legislative requirements. They have expected this activity to fit on the expense side of the balance sheet and have largely failed to view it as a relationship-building exercise that can deliver solutions that stick. They have anticipated little benefit, and so have received none.

We at Twyfords believe the long-term benefits of collaboration stem from the trust, positive relationships and new knowledge created as a result of the process. Trustful relationships, once developed, allow workable governance structures to be established. They enable actions to be planned and implemented quickly and facilitate the efficient delivery of solutions. Other benefits of collaboration include the creation of social capital as well as support for implementation and impetus for further collaborative efforts to achieve agreed goals.

We look at the typical all-or-nothing political debate with some sadness. Too often in politics today both sides seem to be saying, "If we don't get exactly what we want, we are going to make sure you don't either." Such debates often end with a weak compromise, which many assume to be the best possible collaborative outcome.

In these instances, everyone gets something but no one gets everything. This is not collaboration. Collaboration is not about agreement. It's about creation. It's not about arguing or debating. It's about listening and learning. It's about smart leaders creating an environment in which people who care about the consequences of the dilemma co-create solutions that work for them all.

Collaboration is hard work. People want to rush to solutions, so expect some resistance to our philosophy of going slow to go fast. However, establishing the relationships, shared understanding and collective motivation to find a solution that sticks will be worth the effort. The rewards of taking the slower route will manifest themselves in the ability to fast track with confidence as innovation and creativity flows from the collaborators.

So, we stay positive, and are encouraged by stories such as Dale Williams'. We work with our clients to explore their positive experiences where two-way communication, co-operation or possibly even collaboration has worked well in the past.

Drawing from those conversations, we establish the factors that made those experiences successful and ascertain what needs to be done at an individual and organisational level in order to duplicate them. This is the core of what we do and it's a joy when we find a client who 'gets it'. We are excited when clients want what we offer because of the solid commercial benefits that collaborative governance will provide for their organisation.

We hope this book will provide answers to those people who say things like:

"Collaboration means a weak compromise where the only solution which everyone can agree to is based on the lowest common denominator. I want better than that."

"What would you have me do ... get even more people in the room? That means more people who think that if they give an inch, someone will take a mile, so no-one gives an inch!"

We want clients to avoid the type of all-or-nothing approach that screams,

"If I can't get my solution over the line then I won't let them get theirs over either!" The end result of such a process is a weak compromise that nobody believes in.

We look forward to the time when leaders will be willing to step into a conflict transformational process and communicate, cooperate and collaborate using the Power of 'Co'.

The Power of a Good Question

Underpinning many of the stories in this book is a good question. As the saying goes, "Inside each question is a piece of the truth". Collaboration is at its best when we work together to find the questions that hold the truth within. Stories of successful collaboration are inevitably stories about finding the best questions to ask and working together to answer them.

A healthy collaboration fosters and rewards the spirit of inquiry. We have found that one of the keys to supporting this spirit is the art of the strategic question. As we write this book, the ABC aired the documentary entitled *"I Can Change Your Mind About Climate"*. The very title itself reveals the common dynamics of the climate change debate, which is often predicated on one side trying to convince the other how wrong they are.

The spirit of inquiry tells us that a strategic question is the more powerful way to find a path forward. There is a question that holds within itself a smart solution to human impacts on climate and the environment more broadly.

It may be something like, "How do we best honour the natural world and our place within it while providing the highest possible standard of living for all, now and into the future?" And in order to solve this question there will be many smart questions to explore together.

Such questions don't require anyone to be right or wrong. They don't need us to change each other's minds. Rather, strategic questions invite us all to explore the possible together.

The power of a good question is that it goes past difference and allows us to walk together over common ground on our journey to a smart solution. For this reason, good questions lie at the heart of any collaboration.

The Power of 'Co' starts at the Top

Smart Leaders must express, model, and reinforce collaboration for the Power of 'Co' to truly deliver the exponential benefits that we at Twyfords know are possible.

Smart leaders must *Express* the new principles for collaboration, *Model* the collaborative behaviour required, and most importantly *Reinforce* the collaborative methodology and its associated necessary behaviours.

Power of 'Co' is an enabler for Smart Leaders to use in defining and establishing the required reinforcement for change.

Many of the case studies we have recalled in the book have enjoyed a common thread. They have featured a leader or a champion who not only believed in the Power of 'Co', but who more importantly understood their stakeholders well enough to know what behaviours to reinforce to ensure that collaboration went beyond compliance or gestures of goodwill.

In these cases, the Power of 'Co' became the new and only way of working with stakeholders to implement the required change.

It's our contention that once the Power of 'Co' has been experienced, it is difficult to work in any other way. Any other approach seems to engender too much chance and risk. This is not Smart Leadership. The upside of using the Power of 'Co' is that it enables the Smart Leader to tap into and reinforce the latent innovation capacity that resides within all organisations and its stakeholders.

We see the Power of 'Co' as being able to reduce risk. We see it as having the power to release innovation by a co-efficient of ten (x10). Therefore, the *Co-efficient of Collaboration* makes good business sense.

Leaders with the Power of 'Co' recognise that common alternatives to conflict management such as conflict avoidance, outright confrontation or weak compromises present just as much of a challenge, though far fewer opportunities to create real change.

It takes smart leaders with the Power of 'Co' to make a commitment to collaborate. It takes a lot of courage to take that essential step. The work of collaboration binds the collaborators together through shared experiences, shared knowledge around each other's strengths and weaknesses and positive negotiations.

Through successful collaboration, a welcoming and productive environment eventuates and leadership becomes less of an issue. Everybody becomes a leader. Each will have a decisive role to play. Everyone is part of the solution. The more a leader or sponsoring organisation appears open to this approach, the more others will be encouraged to participate.

Our experiences have taught us that collaborative governance works. It works as a means of establishing, understanding and interpreting conversations around complexity and highlighting the types of interactions that need to take place. It gets results. It's not rocket science. It just respects people, expects them to step into dilemmas and then explore and solve them in collaboration with others.

In Chapter One we looked at the Power of 'Co' and its ability to create positive change in society by facilitating an understanding of what makes a problem complex and by providing a means of implementing an unprecedented, qualitatively different approach to creating enduring solutions.

In Chapter Two we explored the Paradox of Power and the challenge for today's leaders including elected representatives, corporate directors, executives, and in fact anyone with power to make decisions that affect others. We offered an explanation of the paradox and offered Smart Power as a new approach. Smart Power is shared power.

We suggest that leaders who share their power, who co-create goals with those who are to achieve them, who share the dilemmas with those who can help solve them, and who provide a supportive environment in which problems can be solved collaboratively, become leaders others wish to follow.

Smart leaders using the Power of 'Co':
- believe in the capacity of people to build lasting solutions and create more enduring solutions than leaders or experts alone;
- believe that enough people working together have the potential to create wise solutions;
- can tap into positive experiences of success and the strengths of individuals creating energy, enthusiasm and positive relationships with stakeholders;
- have constant curiosity and a genuine desire to learn from others to deepen a shared understanding;
- have a determination to work for as long to find enduring solutions together.

In Chapter Three we explained the backwards or reverse logic of each of the steps in the Collaborative Governance process, using it to describe how the steps build the essential foundations of commitment, co-definition and co-design. We illustrated how the steps connect people to each other and build energy, trust, enthusiasm and cooperation to achieve the ultimate goal of collaboration and solution co-creation.

In Chapters Four, Five, Six, Seven and Eight we described in detail each of the five steps of Collaborative Governance; a veritable road map for harnessing the Power of 'Co' in many different situations.

A last word...
The Power of 'Co' is the power of respectful conversations about things that matter to us. Twyfords' Collaborative Governance model is, for us, the structure in which those conversations take place. While it is easy to find many examples where collaboration hasn't been done well, we know that

the art of working together to achieve a common aim is as old as humanity itself.

Indeed, our intention in writing this book was in part to celebrate the powerful faculty for collaboration that teams, organisations, communities and nations so clearly demonstrate.

We believe in collaboration and the value of collaborative governance in supporting people to work together. Our clients have shown us that with appreciative mindsets, smart leaders and processes that are appreciative, informative, deliberative and iterative, we can work together to find enduring solutions to even our most complex dilemmas.

References

Books

Covey, Stephen R *The 7 Habits of Highly Effective People*. Melbourne, Australia: The Business Library 1990

Kahneman, Daniel *Thinking Fast and Slow*. New York: Farrer, Straus and Giroux, 2011

Kaner Sam, Lind Lenny, Toldi Catherine, Fisk Sarah and Berger Duane *Facilitator's Guide to Participatory Decision-Making*. San Francisco: Jossey-Bass 2007

McKay, Hugh *What Makes Us Tick*. Australia: Hachette 2110

Putnam, Robert D *Bowling Along: The Collapse and Revival of American Community*. New York: Simon & Schuster 2000

Schrage, Michael *Shared Minds*. New York: Random House 1990

Semler, Richardo *Maverick*. London: Arrow, 1994

Surowiecki, James *The Wisdom of Crowds*. Great Britain: Little, Brown 2004

Susskind Lawrence and Field Patrick *Dealing with an Angry Public*. New York: The Free Press 1996

Tanner, Lindsay *Sideshow: Dumbing Down Democracy*. Australia: Scribe Publications, 2011

Diagrams

Implementation Management Associates. AIM Methodology – Key Concept Defining Corporate Culture

Snowden, Dave. The Cynefin Framework, 1999

Articles
Ancona Deborah, Malone Thomas W, Orlikowski Wanda J, Senge Peter M. *In Praise of the Incomplete Leader.* Boston, USA: Harvard Business Review 2007

Bisley, Alastair *Note on Collaboration.* New Zealand 2011

Gray, Barbara. *Conditions Facilitating Interorganizational Collaboration.* Pennsylvania, USA: Sage Journals Human Relations 1985

Leo, Denise *Collaboration vs. C-Three (Cooperation, Coordination, and Communication).* New York: Rensselaerville Institute 2010

Quotes
Fishkin, James Professor, Stanford University - Originated the concept of Deliberative Polling® in 1988.

People
Carson, Lyn, is a Professor in Applied Politics at the Centre for Citizenship and Public Policy, University of Western Sydney and a Director of the newDemocracy Foundation.

Cooperrider, David Ph.D, a founder and board member of the Taos Institute and is a Professor and Chairman of the Department of Organisational Behaviour at the Weatherhead School of Management at Case Western Reserve University in Cleveland, USA. He is widely recognised as the "thought leader" of Appreciative Inquiry.

Lederach, John Paul is Professor of Practice for International Peacebuilding with the Joan B. Kroc Institute for International Peace Studies at the University of Notre Dame. He works as a practitioner-scholar, providing facilitation, mediation and training/education, with extensive experience at national and community levels in North and Latin America, Africa, Southeast and Central Asia

About Twyford Consulting

About Twyfords

Twyfords is a team of consultants with a long history of working with people both inside and outside organisations, who share a passion for collaboration. Twyfords have been operating for over 20 years from a base in Wollongong, NSW, Australia.

We have always taken a Capacity Building approach to our work, seeking to enable our clients to do the work they need to do by building their Collaborative Practice.

Our approach to work is Appreciative and Deliberative and encourages shared learning. We provide strategic advice to our clients. Experience has taught us that we make the greatest difference in the world when we work with decision-makers to build their organisational readiness to collaborate with their stakeholders.

We do this strategic work by building relationships with our clients, understanding their needs and working closely with them as they collaborate with their stakeholders to help find enduring solutions to complex dilemmas. We believe that conversations build relationships and that relationships are an essential ingredient of enduring solutions.

The process our clients apply is our Collaborative Governance approach. This five-step process is our road-map for enduring solutions to complex dilemmas.

We work with local, state and federal government, and the private sector. Our expertise is in governance, decision-making, collaboration, strategic stakeholder engagement and the co-creation of wise, enduring solutions.

Our approach is based on the concepts of Appreciative Inquiry which tells us that better outcomes are achieved when we focus on what works well rather than on gaps, barriers and deficiencies. We take this approach to organisational change and to all our work with stakeholders.

We also apply an Appreciative Approach to our work with clients. We realise that the best learning comes from "doing" and we support our clients to learn and apply new collaborative ways of working. We are a team who share a vision and enjoy working with clients to realise that vision.

We believe that people are part of the solution and our work is about helping create better solutions by working with people.

About the Authors

Vivien Twyford BA Grad Dip Com: Vivien was the founding partner of Twyfords in 1988. Having developed a specialty in the area of public participation, Vivien has for the past 25 years designed and implemented stakeholder participation programs around some very sensitive projects. More recently Vivien was part of the Twyfords' collaborative process which developed a new model that we call Collaborative Governance - a way of working with diverse stakeholders to co-create solutions to our most controversial dilemmas - a process urgently needed in today's complex world.

John Dengate BMet: John focuses on current public issues – the "wicked problems" that are frustrating clients – both in the private and public sector. He has the ability to see what is less visible to others and elicits responses via questions that draw a more complete picture of what is really going on. He facilitates the collaborative design of approaches which tackles those underlying issues. He works with ordinary but vexed situations, understands them, designs and delivers exceptional results via the people who are part of that situation.

Max Hardy BSocSc Assoc Dip Social Welfare: Since joining Twyfords in 1997 Max helped establish the International Association for Public Participation Australasia. With a particular interest in Deliberative Democracy and Appreciative Inquiry, he has developed innovative models for community engagement covering a range of projects, including those with a social planning emphasis as well as infrastructure/natural resources management projects.

Stuart Waters Bsc (Hons) MA (Journ): Stuart has a strong technical background in the life sciences and sustainability. He takes this knowledge to his work with people, groups and organisations where he uses deliberative processes to create better outcomes. Stuart is an experienced facilitator, trainer and communicator, with a particular interest in applying deliberative processes to issues of complexity and sustainability.

Contributing Author
Tania Jones BCompSc MACom (Hons): Tania has more than 20 years' experience with global organisations and management consulting practices. In her time at Twyfords Tania made valuable contributions to this book.